THE BEDFORD SERIES IN HISTORY AND CULTURE

The McGuffey Readers

Selections from the 1879 Edition

Related Titles in

THE BEDFORD SERIES IN HISTORY AND CULTURE

Advisory Editors: Natalie Zemon Davis, Princeton University
Ernest R. May, Harvard University

Schools and Students in Industrial Society: Japan and the West, 1870–1940
Peter N. Stearns, *Carnegie Mellon University*

Looking Backward, 2000–1887 by Edward Bellamy
Edited with an Introduction by Daniel H. Borus, *University of Rochester*

How the Other Half Lives by Jacob A. Riis
Edited with an Introduction by David Leviatin

The Souls of Black Folk by W. E. B. Du Bois
Edited with an Introduction by David W. Blight and Robert Gooding-Williams, both of *Amherst College*

Muckraking: Three Landmark Articles
Edited with an Introduction by Ellen Fitzpatrick, *University of New Hampshire*

Women's Magazines 1940–1960: Gender Roles and the Popular Press
Edited with an Introduction by Nancy A. Walker, *Vanderbilt University*

American Social Classes in the 1950s: Selections from Vance Packard's THE STATUS SEEKERS
Edited with an Introduction by Daniel Horowitz, *Smith College*

Brown v. Board of Education: A Brief History with Documents
Waldo E. Martin Jr., *University of California, Berkeley*

THE BEDFORD SERIES IN HISTORY AND CULTURE

The McGuffey Readers

Selections from the 1879 Edition

Edited with an Introduction by

Elliott J. Gorn

Miami University (Ohio)

BEDFORD/ST. MARTIN'S Boston New York

For Bedford/St. Martin's
History Editor: Katherine E. Kurzman
Developmental Editor: Ellen Kuhl
Production Editor: Heidi L. Hood
Marketing Manager: Charles Cavaliere
Editorial Assistant: Thomas Pierce
Production Assistants: Elizabeth Remmes and Arthur Johnson
Copyeditor: Lisa Wehrle
Text Design: Claire Seng-Niemoeller
Indexer: Anne Holmes of EdIndex
Cover Design: Richard Emery Design, Inc.
Cover Art: From the title page of *McGuffey's First Eclectic Reader,* ed. William Holmes McGuffey (Cincinnati: Van Antwerp, Bragg and Co., 1877).
Composition: ComCom
Printing and Binding: Haddon Craftsmen

President: Charles H. Christensen
Editorial Director: Joan E. Feinberg
Director of Editing, Design, and Production: Marcia Cohen
Managing Editor: Elizabeth M. Schaaf

Library of Congress Catalog Card Number: 97-81287

Manufactured in the United States of America.

2 1 0 9 8
f e d c b a

For information, write: Bedford/St. Martin's, 75 Arlington Street, Boston, MA 02116 (617-426-7440)

ISBN: 0-312-13398-7 (paperback)
ISBN: 0-312-17766-6 (hardcover)

Acknowledgments

Selections from the 1879 McGuffey readers are from the Walter Havighurst Special Collection, King Library, Miami University, Oxford, Ohio.

ILLUSTRATIONS

Pages 6, 10, 26, 30: Reprinted courtesy of the Walter Havighurst Special Collection, King Library, Miami University, Oxford, Ohio.

Page 15: Photo by J. Larry Helton Jr., reprinted courtesy of the Society for the Preservation of Ohio One Room Schools, Middletown, Ohio.

Page 20: Reprinted courtesy of the Smith Collection, Lane Public Library, Oxford, Ohio.

Foreword

The Bedford Series in History and Culture is designed so that readers can study the past as historians do.

The historian's first task is finding the evidence. Documents, letters, memoirs, interviews, pictures, movies, novels, or poems can provide facts and clues. Then the historian questions and compares the sources. There is more to do than in a courtroom, for hearsay evidence is welcome, and the historian is usually looking for answers beyond act and motive. Different views of an event may be as important as a single verdict. How a story is told may yield as much information as what it says.

Along the way the historian seeks help from other historians and perhaps from specialists in other disciplines. Finally, it is time to write, to decide on an interpretation and how to arrange the evidence for readers.

Each book in this series contains an important historical document or group of documents, each document a witness from the past and open to interpretation in different ways. The documents are combined with some element of historical narrative—an introduction or a biographical essay, for example—that provides students with an analysis of the primary source material and important background information about the world in which it was produced.

Each book in the series focuses on a specific topic within a specific historical period. Each provides a basis for lively thought and discussion about several aspects of the topic and the historian's role. Each is short enough (and inexpensive enough) to be a reasonable one-week assignment in a college course. Whether as classroom or personal reading, each book in the series provides firsthand experience of the challenge—and fun—of discovering, recreating, and interpreting the past.

Natalie Zemon Davis
Ernest R. May

Preface

From their first appearance in 1836 until their popularity began to diminish at the end of the nineteenth century, McGuffey's Eclectic Readers were the most widely read books in America, second only to the King James Bible. Tens of millions of American children learned the fundamentals of literacy from them. More, these compilations of essays, poems, biblical passages, speeches, and fiction aimed to mold childrens' behavior, their morals, and their outlook on life. Few if any works more deeply shaped American life.

Yet the McGuffey readers have fallen on hard times; indeed, they have grown so out of favor that now they are difficult to obtain. This volume helps remedy that situation. The Bedford edition offers a generous sampling from the 1879 McGuffeys, when the readers reached the height of their popularity. The selections reprinted here represent all of the subjects and genres found in the original texts. Today's students reading this volume will come away with a strong sense of nineteenth-century American culture as it was shaped in thousands of classrooms across the land.

Lessons in the original McGuffeys were grouped according to level of difficulty, ranging from the first monosyllabic words at the beginning of the first reader through selections from Shakespeare in the sixth. However, because contemporary students will use the Bedford edition not to learn grammar and spelling but to learn about American culture, a thematic approach is taken. The selections reprinted here—which comprise roughly one-fifth of the contents of the 1879 edition—are grouped into a dozen broad categories such as virtues and vices, childhood, the work ethic, men and women, literature, and history.

The twelve categories emphasize some of the main themes found in the original readers. But these themes are a modern reconfiguring of the materials, not a replication of the original plan of the 1879 edition. Certainly other categories would be possible. Dividing the selections into a dozen main themes helps bring coherence to very diverse materials. In no sense, however, do these categories exhaust the possibilities for understanding the meanings of the readers. On the contrary, the McGuffey readers were so powerful and so popular because they encompassed such a wide range of ideas, ideas that flowed into each other within a mainstream American ideology. It is the connections between themes—the unfolding of American history as a chapter in Christian history, for example, the relationship between virtues and vices, education as preparation for the world of work, or good character being defined in part by gender—that make the McGuffey readers such an interesting historical source.

ACKNOWLEDGEMENTS

Bedford Books has provided a fine home for this work. Charles Christensen, Joan Feinberg, Niels Aaboe, Katherine Kurzman, and especially Thomas Pierce all made the way easier. Once a manuscript was completed, Heidi Hood, Lisa Wehrle, and Ellen Kuhl provided countless excellent suggestions for the final draft. The outside readers—William J. Reese at the University of Wisconsin–Madison, Susan E. Gray at Arizona State University, John Mayfield at Samford University, and John P. Daly at Louisiana Tech University—offered encouragement, insight, and much-needed criticism. At Miami University, Andrew Cayton read an early version of the essay and helped me understand the context in which William Holmes McGuffey worked, Mary Cayton gave good counsel on nineteenth-century intellectual history, and Peter Williams offered important advice along the way. Kate Rousmaniere of Miami's School of Education provided substantial intellectual assistance regarding the history of education. More, she did what only true friends will do: She listened to me babble on and on about this project. Martin Miller and the staff at Miami University's Special Collections were unstinting in their aid. The staff and collections at the Newberry Library in Chicago also were very important to the final work. Thanks to Larry Helton of the Society for the Preservation of Ohio One-Room Schools, and to Valerie Elliot and the Smith Collection at the Lane Public Library, Oxford, Ohio, for aid in finding important photographs of nineteenth-century schools. Gerry McCauley, as always, came through on getting the work published. And Lisa Vollendorf made life good as I finished the project.

My daughter Jade attended seventh and eighth grades at Talawanda Middle School in Oxford while I worked on this edition. Even though it is hard not to admire the intellectual and moral earnestness of the old readers, I am grateful that her education was much more rich and varied than that offered in the days of the McGuffeys. Watching Jade in school reminded me how important education truly is, yet how difficult a time parents have always had figuring out what is best for their children.

Finally, this book is dedicated to three of my teachers: Will Green, who taught me in high school that I should consider becoming an historian; Lawrence Levine, who taught me early in my college career why to be one; and David Brion Davis, who, when I was in graduate school, taught me how.

Elliott J. Gorn

Contents

THE BEDFORD SERIES IN HISTORY AND CULTURE

The McGuffey Readers

Selections from the 1879 Edition

PART ONE

Introduction: Educating America

THE McGUFFEY READERS

McGuffey's Eclectic Readers taught millions of American children how to read and write during the nineteenth century. These textbooks—anthologies really, of essays, poems, speeches, and stories—offered students a shared cultural outlook, a common set of values, beliefs, and assumptions. The power of the McGuffeys lingered long into adulthood.

Consider author Herbert Quick's reminiscences of the McGuffeys: "That coldness toward books, that absence of love for them . . . was almost universal," he recalled of his boyhood in rural Iowa during the 1860s and 1870s. "My father never read anything. . . . We had no books . . . no time for anything save the drudgery of the farm." Yet during his lifetime, Quick made himself into a highly literate man. He became a teacher, school principal, lawyer, mayor of Sioux City, Iowa, magazine editor, and author of a dozen volumes on history, politics, and literature.[1]

Quick attributed his awakening to the McGuffey readers. "These textbooks constitute the most influential volumes ever published in America," he wrote in his 1925 autobiography. "They were our most popular reading books for generations."[2] Quick acknowledged that the McGuffeys were not an ideal way to learn. They were full of heavy-handed moral advice and religious instruction. Their tone was oppressively didactic. And in the tiny district school that Quick attended, they were vehicles of mind-deadening memorization and recitation.

But the McGuffeys opened whole worlds to him. For the first time in his life he read literary giants like William Shakespeare, John Milton, and Alexander Pope; he even recalled the speeches of Daniel Webster. "A small ration, these McGuffey Readers, for an omnivorous mind; but by no means a negligible one." Quick found that his brief encounters with the great authors prepared him for more substantial ones: "I felt as one who meets in after years a charming person with whom he has had a chance encounter on the train. I had already met the gentleman. I could say as I opened my Shakespeare, my Milton or my Byron, 'Why, don't you remember our meeting away back on the farm in that old book with the front cover torn off? . . . You're no stranger to me."[3]

Quick's experiences with the McGuffeys were replicated countless times across America. These readers were by far the most popular American schoolbooks, the ones that others imitated. Textbooks competed in a very tough marketplace, and publishers went to great lengths to sell them. From their first publication in 1836 through the two major revisions of 1857 and 1879, the McGuffeys outsold all the rest.[4]

Precise figures are unavailable, but sales estimates exist. Louis Dilman, president of the American Book Company in the early twentieth century, guessed that his company printed the following numbers of McGuffeys: from 1836 through the 1840s, 7 million copies; during the 1850s and 1860s, 40 million; in the 1870s and 1880s, 60 million; between 1890 and 1920, 15 million. Dilman's total, 122 million copies, is certainly an overestimate. His 1870–1890 figure of 60 million books yields an average of 3 million copies per year, while Harvey Minnich, a student of the McGuffey phenomenon, believed that in their peak year of 1880, 1.7 million readers were sold. Nevertheless, if we cut Dilman's estimate by more than half, we still have total sales of over 50 million copies. Keeping in mind that these books were handed down within schools and among friends and families, it is clear that outside of the King James Bible, the McGuffey readers were the most widely read books in nineteenth-century America. Indeed, the McGuffeys arguably were the most influential manifestation of American popular culture of the era.[5]

The reasons underlying their popularity are complex. Certainly the readers' selections reinforced a satisfying and convincing image of America. They depicted an idealized version of mainstream, white, middle-class, Protestant American culture. Rarely did the readers portray blacks or Native Americans, the rich or poor (who, if included, were on their way out of poverty), or non-Protestants (especially Catholics). The McGuffeys—in addition to introducing generations of school children to literacy and the rudiments of history and literature—taught a distinct American ideology that helped define the very meaning of the nation, even as they excluded other, more encompassing visions. God, the readers seemed to say, sanctioned American nationhood; piety and patriotism flowed together. The McGuffey readers expressed a powerful American mythology, a cluster of ideas and emotions—centered around protestantism, individualism, and patriotism—that were elevated to mystical faith in the nation's destiny.[6]

These textbooks provided less a depiction of how Americans lived than a revelation of their hopes. Of course, not everyone believed everything they found in the readers. Even school children were not mere sponges; often they read critically, disregarding or rejecting things that their experience rendered suspect. The Huck Finns of the world were not easily "civilized." Still, the readers embodied a consensus of values that a powerful group of Americans—Protestant, white, middle-class—taught their children. The McGuffeys not only explained the world to students, they made a particular set of assumptions, beliefs, and values seem palpable, even inevitable. And children who learned these lessons well grew into a society that rewarded them. As much as any other historical source, these textbooks take us to the ideological heart of America.

The selections in this volume are from the 1879 edition of the readers, the one that appeared at the height of the McGuffeys' popularity, at the moment when they exercised their greatest influence. There were three major editions of the readers, the original compiled by William Holmes McGuffey (his first and second readers appeared in 1836, the third and fourth in 1837), a thorough revision in 1857, and another in 1879. By then, over half of the selections in the original readers were replaced by new material. McGuffey himself was not consulted about the revisions; the texts had become the sole property of their publishers, who decided to hire professional editors and educators to make the changes. While much of the same material remained throughout the decades, the later McGuffeys became a little sunnier in tone, less concerned with the perils of life and the afterlife, and more optimistic about the possibilities of finding heavenly salvation and worldly success. Such changes paralleled the expansive, even aggressive tone of American society late in the nineteenth century. But let us begin at the origins of the McGuffey readers.

AMERICA'S SCHOOLMASTER

The first Eclectic Readers (later published as McGuffey's Eclectic Readers) were strikingly somber. They reflected not only education's seriousness of purpose, but also the solemn personality of their compiler. William Holmes McGuffey was born September 23, 1800, on the western edge of Pennsylvania, near Washington County. His paternal grandparents had migrated to the southeastern part of the state twenty-five years earlier from Scotland. The family was of devout Presbyterian stock, rural people whose desire for land and for religious community had brought them to America. McGuffey's grandfather Billy served in the American Revolutionary War, after which he moved his family to western Pennsylvania with a group of like-minded religious worshipers when the government opened up new frontier lands.[7]

Billy's son Alexander—William's father—helped his parents establish their new homestead and later served as a scout in the Indian wars. He then married Anna Holmes, daughter of one of the wealthiest and most cultured families in Washington County. Soon Alexander sought land for his own growing family (William would eventually have ten siblings) and in 1802 he moved his family to Ohio's Western Reserve, in the northeastern part of the state. Although McGuffey's ancestors migrated widely in the Old Northwest, then, their lives were dominated by the recurrent themes of seizing Native American territory, staking claims, clearing new land, establishing farms, and maintaining a tightly communal religious life among families of like-minded Presbyterians.[8]

Alexander's young son William developed a love of learning that probably stemmed from several sources. The devout Presbyterianism of his family certainly emphasized the importance of each individual's ability to read the Word of God. McGuffey's mother, whose relatives were known for their culture and learning, encouraged young William's interest in education. Perhaps William, being the eldest son on an isolated farm, felt so burdened with work that he sought any possible avenue of escape. Whatever the specific influences, McGuffey was enrolled at an early age in a subscription school (where neighbors agreed to retain and pay a teacher to instruct their children) six miles from his home. There he studied with Presbyterian minister William Wick, lived with his master's family, and helped work their farm. By age fourteen, McGuffey was certified by Wick to teach on his own. He opened a subscription school at Calcutta, Ohio, where forty-eight students from twenty-three local families attended his four-month sessions.[9]

Soon McGuffey was back in school, preparing for the ministry at Old Stone College in Washington, Pennsylvania, under Reverend Thomas Hughes. For two years he lived with the Hughes family, doing chores and church-related work to earn his keep. At age twenty, McGuffey enrolled at Washington College, where he lived with President Andrew Wylie, a thirty-year-old Presbyterian minister. He graduated from Washington with specialities in ancient languages and philosophy. Again McGuffey went back to teaching, this time in a converted smokehouse in Paris, Kentucky. It was there that he met Reverend Robert Hamilton Bishop, a professor at Transylvania College who had just been named president of Miami University. Bishop offered McGuffey the job of professor of ancient languages at the new institution.[10]

So in 1826, after years of living and learning in the homes of his minister educators and mentors, twenty-six-year old William Holmes McGuffey moved to Oxford, Ohio. Chroniclers of this era have described Oxford and the surrounding territory as primitive backwoods, practically wilderness. Indeed, Andrew Wylie wrote to McGuffey from Washington, Pennsylvania, that he wished his old friend had been able to settle "in a more civilized part of the world."[11]

This depiction is exaggerated. Travel between Oxford and the boom town of Cincinnati (thirty-five miles to the south) was relatively easy and routine by horse and boat. While Oxford had only five hundred inhabitants when McGuffey arrived, the town was heavily settled by Presbyterians, and the college had strong ties to that church, along with the network of social and missionary institutions it had spread into the West. Miami was quite progressive in its curriculum, and by the mid-1830s, as McGuffey compiled his readers, the school had seven full-time faculty members and nearly 250 students. Indeed, it was, after Transylvania, the most prominent college west of the Appalachians.[12]

McGuffey carved out a comfortable life for himself at Miami. Like his father before him, he married into a prosperous family. McGuffey's father-in-law, Judge Isaac Spinning, was the owner of a nine hundred-acre farm near Dayton. By 1833, with money from Judge Spinning's estate, the young professor and his wife Harriet built one of the finest houses in Oxford, a structure worth about $1,800. The new home showed that money and status were very much on McGuffey's mind. Indeed, one of the most striking things about the letters between McGuffey and his friends—mostly other young faculty members, ministers, and his former mentors—is how little they wrote about religious matters (though McGuffey was ordained in 1829), pedagogy, or intellectual issues. Instead, they wrote to each other about academic politics, about their ambitions for moving on, and about securing better paying and higher status jobs. All were growing up with the territory and hoping for personal advancement.[13]

Men like McGuffey were not unusual, and towns like Oxford merely partook of a larger pattern of economic development. By the end of the first third of the nineteenth century, the Ohio country had become part of a system of national and even international markets. The fourth most populous state by 1825, Ohio witnessed a spirit of reform and educational progress, an explosion of canal and road building, and a proliferation of voluntary societies where elite men and women attempted to guide society. Southwest Ohio, where the Miami and Ohio Valleys came together near Cincinnati,

William Holmes McGuffey, from a daguerreotype taken a few years after he compiled his first readers.

enjoyed particularly strong in-migration and agricultural development, and so witnessed unusually rapid social and economic change.[14]

The expansion of the market economy—in which farmers and tradesmen produced less of their goods for home consumption and more of them to sell at market price, often to distant buyers—put Ohio at the mercy of a highly erratic business cycle. The new scramble for wealth, the unpredictability of fortunes in an era of panics and depressions, and the speculative frenzies of the early nineteenth century, all convinced many local leaders that restraining men's selfish passions should take precedence over maximizing individual freedom. State and local governments, as well as courts, reform societies, and schools, needed to redouble their efforts, not merely by coercing men but by offering blandishments, moral lessons, and organizational structures for channeling individual efforts into socially responsible means to success.

The common school movement, which mushroomed during the middle decades of the nineteenth century in Ohio and throughout the country, grew out of this context. The population of school-aged children expanded rapidly, as did the number of free, universally available (except for blacks, Native Americans, and sometimes Catholics) locally run primary schools. It was hoped that such schools would not only educate children, they would also open up economic opportunities for the talented, they would teach moral lessons, piety, and a sense of community.[15]

McGuffey was well connected with many of the people who were creating new cultural institutions to help guide the Cincinnati and Miami Valley region. He belonged to influential reform societies such as the Western Literary Institute, an organization of prominent educators who wished to build a superior system of public schools in Ohio. He was asked for his advice on matters such as appointments of local school superintendents and teachers. One important connection was McGuffey's friendship with the Beecher family. Lyman Beecher was perhaps the most prominent minister in early nineteenth-century America. His daughter Catharine was renowned as an educator and as a writer of advice books for women; it was she the Cincinnati publishing firm of Truman and Smith first contacted to do a series of school readers. She recommended McGuffey instead. Writer Harriet Beecher Stowe, Catharine's younger sister, eventually gained enormous fame as the author of *Uncle Tom's Cabin* (1852), but in the 1830s, her husband Calvin Stowe was Ohio's most prominent advocate of an expansive educational policy. McGuffey surrounded himself with important cultural elites like the Beechers, people who intended to shape the life of the booming West. The four readers he assembled in 1836 and 1837 (the fifth and sixth readers were compiled a few years later by his brother, Alexander McGuffey, a Cincinnati attorney) are best understood in this broad context.[16]

Early in the 1830s, then, McGuffey began to collect a wide range of materials for what became his Eclectic Reader series. He wrote many of the pieces in the early readers himself and selected the work of well-known authors for the third and fourth volumes. He gathered local children in his home and tried out some of his lessons on them. By the end of the decade, it was clear that McGuffey had hit on a formula that worked. His selection and presentation of lessons, in combination with the openness of the western market and Truman and Smith's selling abilities, led to very rapid success. Within a few years, sales surpassed all other school texts, and in 1841, the professor's name had become so well known that the publisher changed the title of their series to McGuffey's Eclectic Readers.[17]

GROWING UP WITH THE TERRITORY

By the 1830s, it was a truism that the destiny of the West was the destiny of America. It is not surprising, then, that the fourth reader included Lyman Beecher's "Plea for the West," which was reprinted in subsequent editions under the title "Necessity for Education." "We must educate! We must educate! or we must perish by our own prosperity," insisted Beecher, as he at once glowed over the vast new riches in the lands beyond the Appalachians and warned of their potential for "corrupting abundance." Beecher extolled not the frontier but development. The danger, however, was that without education and religion, success would inaugurate a reign of barbarous materialism. "But what will become of the West," Beecher worried aloud, "if her prosperity rushes up to such a majesty of power, while those great institutions linger which are necessary to form the mind, and the conscience, and the heart of the vast world? It must not be permitted." The solution, Beecher argued, was to disseminate virtue and temper the scramble for wealth through schools, seminaries, and Bible societies. Progress and prosperity must be moderated with self-restraint. The stakes were high. "It took Rome three hundred years to die; and our death, if we perish, will be as much more terrific as our intelligence and free institutions have given us more bone, sinew, and vitality. May God hide from me the day when the dying agonies of my country shall begin." To avoid this fate, America must dispel the forces of darkness—including the rapidly growing Roman Catholic Church—with those of light: Evangelical churches, missions, tract societies, and common schools.[18]

The "Plea for the West" contained many of the themes that McGuffey carefully developed in the readers. Above all, he wanted to set moral boundaries for the materialism he saw around (and within) him. These boundaries would not force a choice between God and Mammon for, as we have seen, McGuffey and his circle were at least as concerned with the latter as the former. Like Beecher, McGuffey wanted to make the world safe for materialism to accept the benefits of prosperity but allay its corrupting tendencies. For McGuffey, the needs of civil society and the demands of religion coincided; industriousness and piety, worldly ambition and eternal salvation were of a piece.[19]

So as McGuffey compiled the first editions of his readers, he worked not only for the thousand dollars offered by Truman and Smith.[20] He worked also to spread a particular outlook, a vision of the world and how it should operate. Along with the basics of grammar, spelling, punctuation, and pronunciation, school children absorbed the central assumptions of evangelical faith and middle-class morality. The former taught them that individuals were responsible for choosing their heavenly destiny, the latter that individuals were responsible for choosing their earthly destiny.[21]

McGuffey and supporters like Beecher were part of a much larger movement of reformers and administrators who strove for a national expansion of common schools. Educational innovators like Horace Mann in Massachusetts and Calvin Stowe in Ohio believed that the classroom could provide both morality and opportunity for a burgeoning democratic society. They argued that expansion of common schools for all children pushed forward the frontiers of democracy, Protestantism, and republicanism. Schools that were free, open to all, and led by well-trained teachers, who inculcated ethics as well as reading and writing, would offer models of how individual success and the common good might flow together. By midcentury, reformers' efforts resulted in more centralized state and county control of schools and a shift away from private to public education. Educational journals, teachers' associations, and normal schools (teacher training institutions) all proliferated. Reformers like McGuffey and his friends in the Western Literary Institute proved to be advanced thinkers who caught the trend of the coming decades, for they were the first generation to spur the growth of common schools.[22]

McGuffey's expansiveness regarding educational matters did not seem to apply to other issues, however, and his personality, always rather prickly, grew even more erratic as the readers were published in the 1830s. He soon found himself at loggerheads with the man who hired him, Robert Hamilton Bishop, then president of Miami University. Although Miami was a state-supported institution, it was also a Presbyterian stronghold, with its faculty, trustees, and leaders coming overwhelmingly from that denomination until well after the Civil War. Bishop might be called a liberal for his views that denominational boundaries could be softened, that studies in human society such as history, politics, and social relations should be taught, and that clerics and educators like himself must take a strong stand against slavery. McGuffey seems to have been much more cautious on all of these issues. He certainly avoided entirely the growing abolitionist sentiment of the Ohio Valley, even though many considered Miami to be a hotbed of abolitionism. Moreover, McGuffey received much criticism from his colleagues for his vanity and

Miami University in McGuffey's day.

ambition, because he constantly jockeyed for new titles and honors. Finally, he was accused by other professors of pandering to students, of currying favor with them even as he put on the facade of a strict disciplinarian. By 1836, his colleagues so disliked him that they virtually forced him to resign from Miami.[23]

McGuffey soon became president of the new Cincinnati College, but within three years a nationwide depression and his own ineptitude as an administrator caused that institution to close permanently. Yet before the decade ended, the trustees of Ohio University in Athens offered McGuffey the presidency of their college. These were perhaps the four unhappiest years in his life. The college grounds in rural Athens were treated as common grazing land by local folk; when McGuffey fenced the campus, they responded angrily with epithets and clods of mud. He refused to back down, and their enmity grew when he asked for and received a reappraisal of local property that resulted in a tax increase, benefiting the college but harming the townsfolk. Nor were these good years for the university, as disciplinary problems enveloped more and more students, and faculty labored under a regimen that began with French study at 5:00 A.M. Deeply hated by many in Athens, McGuffey resigned in 1843 and took a job teaching languages at tiny Woodward College in Cincinnati. Two years later, his still strong reputation as a teacher, preacher, and scholar secured him a professorship at the University of Virginia, which he held until his death in 1873.[24]

Perhaps the image of William Holmes McGuffey fleeing Athens, Ohio, a victim not only of circumstance but also of his own Scots-Presbyterian sternness and sense of duty tells us something about what he tried to teach children in the readers. While their contents certainly changed over the years and their tone grew livelier as editors and publishers tailored them for new markets, much of McGuffey's moral rectitude and self-righteousness, which were so much a part of his personality and his culture, always remained in his readers.

THE McGUFFEYS' LESSONS

One way to interpret the McGuffey readers is as a direct expression of a deeply religious sensibility, one that grew out of frontier Christian communities. McGuffey attempted to inculcate religion in children, pure and simple. The selections of Scripture, the prayers, the stories reinforcing obedience to the Ten Commandments, the images of an eternal afterlife were all testaments of faith. The drama of humankind's fall, of Christ's death and resurrection, and of God's grace formed the religious worldview undergirding McGuffey's thinking and that of his circle. This deeply religious frame of reference lasted throughout the life of the readers. To be sure, there was a marked difference between the original McGuffeys the 1836 and the 1879 edition reprinted here. Although McGuffey was never the pure Calvinist that some of his biographers claimed (he clearly believed that human beings exercised control over their eternal fates and that the Lord had not irrevocably made those decisions eons ago), God in the early readers did seem more judgmental, demanding, and ubiquitous than in later editions. Nonetheless, if evangelical Protestantism took on a rosier hue by the late nineteenth century, the emphasis on choosing to be saved, on leading a Christian life, on taking personal responsibility for sin and salvation remained.[25]

Another way to interpret the readers' lessons, seemingly an antithetical one, is to understand texts like the McGuffeys as products of social and economic life, teachers of values that prepared children for an urban-industrial culture. Avoidance of lying and idleness were indispensible to a booming capitalist economy, and diligence was the cardinal virtue of a good employee. To put it more precisely, the readers helped spread the values of a small but growing business class outward to ambitious new men and downward to a growing working class. Even abstention from alcohol, which the readers repeatedly taught, was not an age-old Christian virtue but a new social imperative for an era demanding steady labor habits. The McGuffey readers trained good workers for the marketplace. Certainly these messages were always present, but they grew increasingly prominent by the 1879 edition.[26]

Both of these interpretations of the readers are correct. The McGuffeys did reflect an evangelical viewpoint, did teach that people can take their eternal destiny into their own hands and choose to be saved. McGuffey and the men who revised subsequent editions of his readers molded the remarkably pliable Protestantism of this evangelical era into a powerful social force. Both the public school movement and the church were intimately tied to new problems of class and ideology created by the expansion of the market economy during the nineteenth century; both inculcated the bourgeois ethic of sobriety, steady work, thrift, responsibility, piety, and self-restraint; and both assumed that individuals must be free to determine their own fates on earth and in the hereafter, but that personal aggrandizement must be hedged by moral imperatives. Eternal salvation and economic success required the same sorts of behaviors. Saving souls and providing opportunity were parts of the same process.[27]

Certainly institutions like public schools and missionary societies favored the values of one class over another. Those who were rich and considered respectable exercised a kind of cultural control when they tried to regulate the poorer classes' thoughts and behaviors, even through such seemingly innocuous things as school textbooks. The contents of McGuffeys and other readers were not based on universally accepted ideals. Many Catholics, for example, opposed selections from the King James Protestant Bible in the schools. (Catholic mass was said in Latin.) Catholics often sent their children to their own parochial schools; for Catholic parents, common schools were Protestant schools.[28] Immigrants experienced decades of harsh discrimination in America, sometimes because of their Catholicism (which was seen as aggressive, authoritarian, anti-individualistic), sometimes because of their cultural distinctiveness (Germans continued their old-world language and cultural institutions, for example), and sometimes because of their poverty (especially the Irish who came over in waves during the Great Famine beginning in 1847). Immigrants sought to give their children a distinct identity through their own school texts, such as Gilmour's Catholic National Series, which was commonly used in parochial schools. Gilmour's fifth reader contained many of the same selections found in the McGuffeys, like "The

Blue and the Gray," "The Barefoot Boy," and "Rip Van Winkle," but it also contained pieces like "Catholicity and American Liberty," by Archbishop John Hughes, and "The Power of the Blessed Sacrament," by Reverend Michael Muller.

Not only Catholics felt left out of common schools or affronted by readers like the McGuffeys. African Americans in many districts were systematically excluded from public education or made to attend inferior institutions. For Native Americans, studying in reservation schools taught by missionary teachers using texts like the McGuffeys could seem more like indoctrination and religious persecution than education. Many poorer citizens believed that schools were a tax burden from which others would benefit. Even groups like Norwegian immigrants occasionally opposed the imposition of English on their children.[29]

Men like McGuffey did not see things this way. Stewardship, the responsibility of the well born for the less fortunate, was an age-old tradition among Protestants, many of whom believed that the comfortable classes had an obligation to uplift the poor—morally, spiritually, and educationally. Self-appointed moral stewards saw themselves as champions of a better way of life, one that any sensible person would willingly embrace. They approached the world with tremendous moral certitude and were convinced that their view of things was the right one. Salvation was truly open to all who sought it, and the same individuals would also choose the life of middle-class rectitude. Property and piety formed the foundations of civilization and the cornerstones of American society. Teachers of the cultural beliefs that pervaded the readers saw themselves as bearers of gifts, not as cultural imperialists.[30]

Even as the readers taught grammar and spelling and elocution, then, evangelical and middle-class ideology pervaded the lessons. Children learned the importance of honesty, hard work, and sobriety; they learned obedience to parents and God and the importance of meeting one's obligations; they learned that human beings above all creatures were capable of acquiring knowledge and that this allowed them, indeed obliged them, to improve the world; they learned that honest labor brought prosperity and that property acquired virtuously was a sign of God's approval; they learned to associate men with productive labor, especially labor outside the home, and women with nurturing, child-rearing, and household tasks; and they learned to think of people who were different from themselves (racially, ethnically, or religiously) as less fortunate, even inferior, but mostly invisible.[31]

Perhaps most important, the readers tried to develop in children a sense of conscience, that indispensible moral gyroscope for guiding bourgeois citizens safely through a society extolling individual acquisitiveness.

For an expanding market economy based on the inviolability of contracts, conscience made the pursuit of personal gain orderly and predictable and tempered the chaotic and destructive potential of market society. Fear of God and of parents endowed with His authority were the font of conscience in children, but it was the internalization of values that the McGuffeys ultimately strove for.[32]

A decade and a half after McGuffey compiled the readers, his son Charles attended boarding school, and the advice given from father to son was the same advice the professor tried to pass on in his textbooks. After advising Charles to work on his handwriting (indispensible for work in a law office), McGuffey wrote, "Remember, my dear son, to read a portion of your Bible every day—and do not forget daily . . . to pray to God to keep you from evil, and to prepare you for the duties of life and for the hour of death. Think often of your departed Mother, and often ask yourself how she would advise, and what she would think of any course you are about to pursue." A few months later McGuffey wrote, "Let me remind you of the importance of industry in your studies. . . . Everything depends upon habits formed in youth—this you know, but we are all liable to forget." And a month later McGuffey concluded, "Remember that the way to success is the path of duty."[33]

As a compiler, William Holmes McGuffey and those who subsequently revised his readers were conduits of culture, popularizers of fundamental beliefs. The readers gave crystal-clear expression to bourgeois values for children born into a society more tightly tied to the market economy than ever before. The McGuffeys made pious middle-class ways seem as natural as air and the outlooks of other people, if visible at all, unthinkable.

THE McGUFFEYS' AUDIENCE

From the very beginning and with each subsequent edition, the McGuffeys' greatest popularity was in the Midwest and South, and in rural and small-town schools rather than in major cities. Truman and Smith, as well as later Cincinnati-based publishers Sargent, Wilson and Hinkle (beginning in 1863) had their greatest success in the nation's heartland. Beginning with Truman and Smith, the readers were distributed by smart and aggressive publishers, all of whom had their strongest business contacts close to home, so their sales staffs concentrated their efforts in regional markets. Even when New York's American Book Company brought out the 1879 edition, printing and distribution remained centered in Cincinnati. McGuffey readers never did particularly well in the Northeast,

Sixteen Mile Stand School, Symmes Township, Hamilton County, Ohio. The school, named because the village stood sixteen miles from downtown Cincinnati, was built in 1879, the same year as the McGuffey readers reproduced in this book.

perhaps because there was so much established competition there; indeed, virtually all other early texts were written by New Englanders. Moreover, the McGuffeys' religious and moral conservatism fit the sensibility of the heartland. So while the readers sold well everywhere, it was from the Great Lakes to the Gulf that their popularity was greatest.[34]

The McGuffey readers were not unique among nineteenth-century schoolbooks, but there were important differences between them and their competitors. Perhaps most striking was the absence of diversity in the McGuffeys; the image of America they presented was one of rural ways and ethnic homogeneity. On the issue of slavery, for example, McGuffey readers remained silent throughout the nineteenth century. African Americans, underground railroads, whips and chains, abolitionists, and even the Civil War itself were almost completely ignored. Even compared to other school readers, the McGuffeys presented an especially homogenized picture of America. On these pages, a generous boy might help a poor German family or Native Americans might speak as noble representatives of a race now virtually extinct, but minorities as a living presence in America barely existed. Not that other textbooks were exemplary. Toward the end of the century, they often reproduced standard racial typologies that depicted the alleged hierarchy of human types propagated by the scientific racism of the day—civilized whites, black savages, and others somewhere in between. Ethnic stereotypes abounded: Native Americans were bloodthirsty, Catholics gullible, Jews heartless, and blacks lazy. But children reading from the McGuffeys dwelled in a lily-white world; they scarcely received any information at all that America was a very diverse nation (for an exception, see p. 90).[35]

Such crucial differences aside, the McGuffey readers seem to have sold so well because they managed not to be exceptional, because they captured a broad middle ground. Generally speaking, the McGuffeys' contents conformed quite well to the main contours of other nineteenth-century American textbooks. By the 1879 edition, publishers had learned to find the widest possible audience and to offend the fewest possible purchasers. Textbooks invariably depicted America as nature's nation, so that rurality meant virtue, godliness, health, and happiness. The emphasis was not on wilderness, but on a pastoral middle landscape where humankind blended harmoniously with the land and where the earth gave virtuous tillers of the soil prosperity and independence. While cities represented materialism and corruption, country life stood for wholesome independence. Just like the McGuffeys, a large number of selections from other school readers were either taken directly from the Bible or based on biblical stories. Of course, God had singled out America as His special place. Like the ancient Hebrews, Americans were the chosen people, and the Almighty led men like Christopher Columbus and George Washington on their divinely appointed missions.[36]

The McGuffey readers stressed individual heroism and held up great men such as Benjamin Franklin and William Penn as models for youth to emulate. (Examples of great women, however, were rarely used.) Whereas Europeans often were depicted as bloated aristocrats or bloody revolutionaries, American patriots abhorred luxury and worked for the common good. The great men of history were models of industriousness, frugality, perserverence, and piety; their lives were presented with a lofty moral tone. The McGuffeys' heroes tended to be accomplished in practical fields like politics and science rather than art and literature. By cleaving to the high virtues of diligence, prudence, and honesty, they brought progress to all humankind. The great men's lives also taught lessons of equality; such men did not inherit an exalted social status but accomplished great things purely by dint of their own hard work. The message, of course, was a deeply patriotic one: America gave these men liberty and opportunity, and they gave their talent back to their country, even as they provided models of republican selflessness.[37]

Above all, nineteenth-century schoolbooks contained very conservative messages. Social tensions were largely ignored, and critical thinking was rarely taught. For example, despite a powerful feminist movement during the mid-nineteenth century, school texts generally depicted women in service to men and to their families. Women's role was the domestic one of bringing moral refinement to the American family. Indeed, all of the controversial social movements of the nineteenth century—abolitionism, feminism, socialism, trade-unionism—simply did not exist in school textbooks. Only two social reforms seemed to be on the agenda, the public school movement and the temperance crusade. What textbooks did uphold with mind-numbing regularity was the gospel of work. They taught children not only to work hard but to value labor. Obedience to authority and self-control were highly prized traits in both students and workers. The classroom was a place of discipline, of regimentation, and of preparation for the workplace. Schools taught habit, industriousness, and regularity; they encouraged children to internalize a very cautious bourgeois moral code, to acquire a firm sense of duty, to distrust their impulses, and to build up their capacity for regular and self-denying work. A sense of life's seriousness and of moral gravity pervaded nineteenth-century readers, especially the McGuffeys.[38]

CONTEXTS

It is difficult to read the McGuffey readers today and see them as progressive in their pedagogy, yet in important ways they were precisely that. The child-centered ideas of the educational reformer J. H. Pestalozzi, which stressed the natural goodness of children, were becoming widely accepted by the mid-nineteenth century. Teaching techniques themselves were changing. Especially for young children, traditional methods of teaching stressed learning the alphabet, then memorizing letter combinations and syllables, and finally vocabulary. Progressive pedagogy, on the other hand, emphasized general reading. Through the nineteenth century, English and American teaching increasingly became less rigid; grammar, spelling, pronunciation, and so forth remained important, but educators implicitly recognized that gaining a grasp of language was not an entirely orderly process, that children needed to experiment, and that one learned to read by reading. By early in the century, compendia of short pieces, anthologies like the McGuffeys, became the norm in classrooms, with children being assigned reading geared to their individual levels of accomplishment. Of course, this type of education depended heavily on the skill of the compiler. Publishers of various readers all claimed that their expertise at organizing materials brought students through the learning process at just the right pace.[39]

Despite reforms, learning tended to be a dull experience. In rural and small town schools, a single teacher often was responsible for a roomful of students ranging in age from six to eighteen. By the time of the 1879 McGuffey edition, age-grading had come to many school districts so that children of roughly the same age and ability shared a teacher, classroom, and curriculum. But in both one-room schoolhouses and age-graded districts, memorizing passages, copying out texts in longhand, and reciting poetry and prose with proper elocution were the stuff of daily classroom activity. Teachers grouped their students so that the more advanced ones acted as tutors for the less skilled. At any given time, most students might be sitting at their desks doing slate work, memorizing paragraphs, diagramming sentences, or solving arithmetic problems, while a few others stood before the teacher's desk and demonstrated what they had learned. Throughout the nineteenth century, the spoken word was highly valued, and teachers spent considerable classroom time instructing on proper oratorical skills. In larger classrooms, recitations occurred in unison, as the teacher evaluated her charges.[40]

Even greater change than age-grading was on the rise in public schools, especially those in larger cities and towns. The years of McGuffey readers' greatest popularity were also a time of tremendous expansion in the schools, backed by compulsory attendance laws. In 1830, just before the first edition of the readers appeared, the school enrollment rate (the percentage of children who spent time in school) for whites between the ages of five and nineteen was 35 percent; by 1850, it had topped 50 percent, and in 1870, it was 61 percent. As of 1890, two out of three children enrolled in school. During the years of the McGuffeys' greatest popularity, then, the rate of attendance nearly doubled, and some towns had 90 percent of their children in class. Also during these years, illiteracy nationwide declined from 20 to 13 percent. Moreover, total education expenditures—public and private, state and local—rose 400 percent (adjusted for inflation) between 1850 and 1870. Even high school, which was never part of most students' experience until well into the twentieth century, grew more common, especially for the middle class in commercial cities. By the late nineteenth century, high school attendees were young men and women whose fathers were shopkeepers, professionals, or brokers. The graduates tended to follow in their fathers' footsteps or to become teachers, merchants, or college students. Still, as of 1890, less than 1 percent of the American population received any secondary schooling, whether high school or college.[41]

The middle decades of the nineteenth century saw schools established where they had never been before and education regularized where it had been intermittent. The pattern of school expansion was far from even. Public education spread most rapidly in the Midwest, followed by New England and the Mid-Atlantic states, while the South lagged behind the rest of the nation. Irish and German Catholics preferred their own private schools to public ones, African Americans were largely excluded from classrooms in the South and segregated in the North, and Native Americans found themselves excluded altogether from schools or subjected to heavy missionary efforts. While profound differences in the quality of education remained, the growing system of common schools provided most children with the rudiments of reading, writing, history, geography, and arithmetic. The schools also gave them common background in nondenominational Protestantism and taught the values of punctuality, achievement, competitiveness, and respect for adults. The common schools thus offered children the possibility of sharing a common culture and a set of values that adjusted them to their world as citizens and workers.[42]

Classroom conditions varied enormously from school district to school district, based on wealth and demographics, but some clear patterns

A rural school of the Midwest. Note how the teacher, the superintendent, and the students have positioned themselves.

emerged. Ages eight through thirteen were by far the most common ones for public school attendance. Kindergartens rarely existed, and early schooling that mingled children with strangers was thought to be morally and intellectually dangerous before the age of six or seven. On the other end of the age scale, most early teens had absorbed basic literacy skills and were old enough to enter the labor market. Because in the late nineteenth century males were more likely to work outside the home, girls tended to stay in school a bit longer than boys and were more likely to attend high school. College, however, was mostly a male institution. Rural schools, because of their small size, were usually coeducational; urban public schools were more often segregated by gender.[43]

Another thread uniting all schools—rural, urban, public, private, and religious—was the predominance of women instructors, who comprised roughly three out of five teachers when the 1879 edition of the McGuffey readers was published. Here was a convergence of ideology and practicality. Not only was teaching seen as a nurturing role, but also female teachers earned much smaller salaries than men (anywhere from 40 to 75 percent of male salaries), and school boards were always happy to keep costs down. Since before the Civil War, the "cult of true womanhood" had insisted that females' superior moral nature made them guardians of religion and virtue. Increasingly, men left home to make their livings rather than working in fields outside the house or in a shop downstairs. Women stayed home to provide a "haven in a heartless world" for their families, laboring alongside their husbands less than ever now that workplace and home no longer coincided. The boundaries between labor and family life grew ever sharper. Schools became a halfway house between public and private spheres, and teachers helped prepare students for this increasingly bifurcated social life. Classrooms were surrogate families where not only syntax but ethics and values were taught. Not coincidentally, by 1870 at least half of all teachers were women; by 1900, about three-quarters were. School administration, however, remained a male bastion.[44]

The ties between women and education were so powerful that Horace Mann, the great reformer of the Massachusetts school system, wrote of how he learned to associate learning, literacy, and Christianity with the benevolent nurturing of his mother and sisters. By the late nineteenth century, the common schools were very much a part of women's world; only in high school did disciplinary problems with older boys make that institution a more male-dominated one. (Of course, discipline was a constant issue in the schools, even though the readers depicted a perfect world where obedient children were rewarded and unruly ones punished.) As in the home, women in the classroom allegedly purified morals, upheld ideals of modesty, and taught the virtues of Protestant Christianity and American patriotism; in other words, they helped reproduce bourgeois life. So the schools were part of women's realm, but they operated in the service of new middle-class norms about gender, norms that easily gave men the greatest share of power.[45]

Because men claimed the world of work for themselves, they took most leadership roles in the common school movement. In important respects McGuffey was typical. He came from a middling rural background on the western edge of white settlement and rose socially by dint of hard work and education. All such individuals reproduced their own lives and values in the schools and, despite disagreements among themselves, agreed that the common schools must teach morality: that is, nondenominational Protestantism, the nurturing role of women, the virtues of republicanism, the superiority of American nationalism, and the sanctity of private property and social mobility.[46]

THE HEARTLAND

While the McGuffey readers apparently sold well everywhere in the country except New England, they always remained especially popular in the nation's heartland. From the cultural hearth of Ohio, the readers spread west with the canals and railroads that knit together the market economy of small towns and farms. By the last third of the nineteenth century, McGuffeys were central to the culture of Michigan, Indiana, Illinois, Missouri, Iowa, Wisconsin, and Minnesota, running as far west as the eastern parts of Kansas, Nebraska, and the Dakotas. While not quite as pervasive as in the Midwest, they also sold well south of the Ohio River into what had been the Confederacy.[47]

Yet even as the readers spread with commercial culture, they denied many of the manifestations of that culture. Selections focused on rural and small town life. Cities, technology, immigrants, the poor, religious conflict, racial strife—all barely existed in the readers, even though all had become part of daily life in nineteenth-century America. Horse-drawn buggies more than railroads, family farms instead of staple-crop estates, artisan shops rather than industries filled the McGuffeys. While the older ways certainly still existed when the 1879 edition was published, American society's dash toward modernity was abundantly clear. In an age characterized by government corruption, mounting worries over the power of private businesses, and fears about the growing divisions of rich and poor, the McGuffey readers portrayed America through a thick sentimental haze.[48]

For example, in 1877, two years before the 1879 edition, America experienced the Great Railroad Strike in which thousands of employees, disgusted with wage cuts amidst a deep recession, laid down their tools, stopped the transcontinental railroad for a few days, and with it, much of the American economy. Dozens of employees were killed by government troops, millions of dollars of property destroyed, and some people believed that America was on the verge of class warfare. Yet the McGuffeys persisted in their bucolic vision during, or perhaps in response to, this age of strife. The readers clung to a nostalgia that refused to accept the unpleasant realities of modern social and economic life. But by ignoring how the booming market economy destabilized so much of life, the

McGuffeys softened the face of industrial capitalist society and helped it to escape criticism. Even as social protest and labor unrest mounted in the last decades of the nineteenth century, even as newspapers filled with accounts of poverty and unemployment, even as growing numbers of children went to work in mines and factories, other children still read in the McGuffeys that virtuous hard work was always rewarded.[49]

To a remarkable extent, the very identity of the the nation's heartland was tied to the market culture of capitalism. Power and influence flowed to those who professed the worldview that the McGuffey readers had helped spread. Ethnic and religious minorities, working-class people, and especially all whose way of life seemed disorderly became less than equal in a society constantly proclaiming its devotion to equality. Countless Americans fell outside the charmed circle: immigrants like the mostly Catholic Germans and Irish who arrived in enormous numbers around midcentury with their traditions of conviviality on the sabbath; working men cast adrift from their bosses' watchful eyes as the workplace shifted from the home-based shops to the factories; transient rural working-class members largely excluded from institutions of social control by the seasonal rhythms of their labor; young men who chose to shun piety for the life of male camaraderie; and women, many of whom left the confines of homes and farms to labor in the capitalist marketplace (and indeed, some of whom resorted to selling their bodies as prostitutes to make their living).[50]

Against perceived threats of disorder, the middle class developed an intensely privatized family structure. An emotional life based on internalized mechanisms of guilt, repression, and conscience kept individuals on the straight and narrow. Certainly by the last third of the century, the market economy so dominated mid-America that community–life had to be forged within it. Disparate individuals shared the value of acquisitiveness, but at the heart of commercial life was a simple contradiction: The quest for economic growth could turn predatory without some form of social discipline. The culture that the middle class created and the communities that brought people together sought to engender orderly economic growth and to discourage rapacious self-aggrandizement. Church and school, family and literary societies, booster groups and temperance clubs all helped businessmen, professionals, and shopkeepers to know and trust each other and to create a predictable economic climate. Business, morals, and community were intertwined. Progress and growth became key social goals, even as an aesthetic of nostalgia and sentimentality—in music, in artwork, in literature—sought to deny society's headlong rush into the future.[51]

Despite the efforts of McGuffey and his friends in Cincinnati during the 1830s, public schooling did not become a powerful movement in the nation's heartland until the 1850s, and rapid expansion awaited the end of the Civil War. Initially, funds were limited, and most early settlers had little reason to be interested in education, oriented as they were to their farms and local communities. Indeed, schools represented the larger commercial world that many people feared. Because education served the bourgeois outlook, schools threatened local control; too much book-learning militated against the "common sense" knowledge needed to run a farm. Around midcentury, however, the new transportation system helped bring so many people into the market economy that the middle class began winning its battle for schools, as state after state passed laws authorizing free public education. By the next generation, by the time of the 1879 edition of the McGuffeys, commercial civilization and bourgeois ways had triumphed so completely that free public schools were seen as one of the glories of American culture.[52]

These broad social transformations were reflected in the readers. Perhaps the most important change to occur by the 1879 edition was not the elimination of the older didactic material, but the addition of new passages. These selections leavened the readers with just a bit more humor and drama. But more important than the new lessons aimed at keeping children's interest were the ones that offered literary polish. Pieces by "great" authors appeared with increasing frequency. Such literature not only had a "civilizing" influence on children, it also helped socialize them into the middle class, giving them a common vocabulary and a shared set of cultural symbols. Culture—that is, "high" culture, literature, the arts, the best that was thought and said, as the English critic Matthew Arnold put it—became the common currency for a social stratum that sought to mark its own boundaries and to define the terms of membership in its privileged group. By inculcating gentility, the readers helped the middle class assume a distinct cultural tone.[53]

This refinement of American culture began long before McGuffey compiled his readers. But schools and school texts were a very important part of that process. Parlors in the home where guests might be entertained, books on the shelf to display one's learning, paintings on the wall depicting scenes of beauty and tastefulness, all gave material evidence of people's claims to being genteel, cultivated, not vulgar. Education itself became a possession that allowed one to display refinement and therefore status. The McGuffeys placed so much emphasis on elocution because *how* one spoke had become a marker of social position every bit as much as *what* one said. Gentility, in other words, was one new source of power. The trappings of refined life allowed individuals to reveal their status to each other and to separate themselves from the uncouth. Paradoxically, within this cult of gentility, which had become central to middle-class life during the nineteenth century, lay a sort of democratic impulse: Refinement was something one could acquire through hard work and inner cultivation. Alongside Christian piety and the work habits needed in a capitalist society, the McGuffey readers contributed to the refinement of culture, a refinement that had become an integral part of America's social structure.[54]

PEDAGOGY

By today's teaching standards, the 1879 edition of the McGuffey readers appears rather crude. The introduction to each volume ranges from a few pages to a few dozen, but all contain lists of rules and examples to be mastered by students. Following each introduction are essays, poems, bits of fiction, and biblical passages, all seemingly thrown together at random. The only real organizing principle within and between volumes is the editors' assessment of the selections' difficulty. In volume four, for example, a lesson called "The Tempest" is followed by "The Creator" and then by "The Horse." The logic that places together pieces on meteorology, God, and equine quadrupeds is not based on similar subject matter nor on the literary genre of each piece, but on how challenging these selections would be to students. Within this structure, the pedagogical techniques that the McGuffeys encourage consist of rote mastery of the rules of spelling, grammar, and pronunciation, along with memorizing, reciting, and writing out passages of text in longhand. The readers are not self-reflexive; rarely are questions raised on the meanings or significance of passages.

Because nineteenth-century classes were not always graded according to students' age or depth of knowledge, it is difficult to speak of each reader as the equivalent of a particular modern grade level. The content and format of schoolbooks have changed so drastically that such comparisons become tricky. Roughly, the first four McGuffeys were used in the common schools and brought students to about the level of a middle school education. The fifth and sixth readers were for more advanced work, including high school and college.

McGuffey's First Eclectic Reader was designed to teach children the rudiments of reading. Here the McGuffeys were quite progressive, recommending phonics for the task. Students learned to recognize the sounds associated with particular letters or clusters of letters and to pronounce those sounds as they came across them in words. The first

McGUFFEY'S
FIRST READER
LESSON 1.

dŏg̅ the răn

ă ŏ n d g̅ r th

The dog.

The dog ran.

(7)

First lesson from *McGuffey's First Eclectic Reader,* 1879 edition.

lessons in this reader use two- or three-letter words only. New words are introduced in each subsequent story and are printed at the beginning of the lesson with diacritical markings (long and short vowel sounds, for example) so that children could learn to recognize and pronounce them. The first reader also gives an initial lesson on handwriting. The second reader builds on the foundation laid down by the first. The volume's introduction explains the rudiments of grammar and punctuation, including use of the period, comma, hyphen, exclamation point, and question mark. New words with diacritical markings appear once again at the beginning of each selection. Above all, *McGuffey's Second Eclectic Reader* stresses the importance of oral presentation. The introduction reprints long lists of diphthongs, subvocals, and aspirates to be memorized by children.

Most students probably did not get beyond the third reader. Not only were school terms short and attendance sporadic, but by the time children turned thirteen or fourteen, they were needed to work on farms and in factories, which made anything beyond basic literacy a luxury. The third reader continues the emphasis on elocution, adding to the introduction more elaborate and extensive exercises in the articulation of sounds, including the use of italics to teach students which words to emphasize while reading aloud. Spelling exercises and additional work on punctuation are added to the opening pages, and brief definitions of new words appear at the end of each lesson.

The McGuffey readers were used in schools that usually did not have specialized courses in particular fields of learning (American history, English literature, and so forth). The disciplines we take for granted today were born in American universities at the end of the nineteenth century. Nevertheless, the fourth reader incorporates increasing amounts of material on history and literature and even identifies many of the authors of the various selections with thumbnail biographies, a practice that grew more common with the fifth and sixth readers. While new words are no longer introduced at the beginning of each lesson, the numbers of definitions at the end increase. The fourth reader, like all the others, lays great stress on elocution. In addition to long new lists of subvocals and aspirates, several pages at the beginning of the volume are devoted to correcting errors in articulation. Students are taught to say fir-ma-ment rather than fir'ment, pre-vail instead of pr'vail, cor-por-al and not cor-per-al. The introduction also offers a section of difficult practice sentences to teach clear and distinct speech.

McGuffey's Fifth Eclectic Reader introduces a new focus, as its preface explains: "It has been the object to obtain as wide a range of leading authors as possible, to present the best specimens of style, to ensure interest in the subjects, to impart valuable information, and to exert a decided and healthful moral influence." The emphasis on reprinting authors considered to be literary masters underscored the importance of elocution. Students who had come this far in their educations might well be thinking about careers in teaching, the ministry, law, or politics, all of which demanded eloquence. In addition to its lists of errors in articulation and its pronunciation exercises, the fifth reader introduces new concepts such as tone, accent, voice modulation, poetic pauses, and so forth. To read aloud effectively, the introduction declares, students must not only know a lesson well and identify with the author's position, but must also convey the author's feelings and emotions.

McGuffey's Sixth Eclectic Reader was reserved for that elite group of students who attended high school and even college. History, literature, and moral essays are more abundant than ever. Once again, many lessons begin with mini-biographies of their authors and conclude with definitions of unfamiliar words, as well as literary allusions and explanations of historical references. A whole section of the introduction discusses figures of speech; similes, for example, are to be read in a lower key and more rapidly than the rest of the text. The sixth reader gives advice on voice, pitch, and oral pacing, and on body gestures and carriage. The editors return to the importance of elocution, quoting one unnamed orator that words should be delivered "as beautiful coins, newly issued from the mint, deeply and accurately impressed, perfectly finished; neatly struck by the proper organs, distinct in due succession, and of due weight." Not only are words like money, the introduction continues, but good speech, like good breeding, must be taught at a very early age. No doubt it was unconscious, but comparing proper speech with money and elocution with good breeding made explicit that education, especially at the level of the sixth reader, had as much to do with social class and professional status as with learning to read and write the English language.

As teaching tools, the McGuffeys' popularity gave them an authority lacking in other textbooks. They provided generations of students with a lingua franca, however biased or contrived, that went beyond common readings to a shared set of morals, aesthetics, and beliefs. The readers were successful in teaching students rudimentary knowledge, not because they were pedagogically sophisticated but because parents and teachers enforced memorization and recitation as the keys to learning. However, judged by more modern-day educational standards—teaching students to think for themselves, to recognize the diversity of their world, or to see life as filled with moral ambiguity and aesthetic possibilities—the readers were not so successful. Indeed, these newer standards ran contrary to the McGuffeys' goals.

THE McGUFFEYS TODAY

In his fine work, *Making the American Mind,* the historian Richard Mosier explores how the McGuffey readers melded Christian values with middle-class ideals to form a blueprint for American culture. The genius of the McGuffeys, he argues, was to make this merger of social and economic imperatives with a religious sensibility all but seamless. Mosier, however, writes too much as if the readers spoke for a single, united American culture. His book is part of a larger body of work written in the 1950s and 1960s that tends to see Americans as a more unified people than they actually were. It is more accurate to view the readers as an expression of one particular group, albeit a large and powerful one, as a set of symbols and ideas whose appeal spread widely over the years.[55]

Men like William Holmes McGuffey struggled to establish the common schools and to put into children's hands textbooks that would reinforce the middle-class Protestant worldview. They struggled because there was nothing obvious or inevitable about the causes they advocated. Indeed, as we have seen, the nineteenth-century schools largely excluded blacks, slighted Catholics, ignored the needs of working-class and rural people, kept women out of leadership roles, and taught Native Americans that they were inferior. It is only in the twentieth century that many Americans look back with nostalgia to the assumed cultural unity represented by one-room schoolhouses filled with children reciting lessons from McGuffey readers. That unity was always a myth; American culture was never so monolithic.

Still, the McGuffey readers gave powerful expression to important ideological positions. The students who read these pages a century ago were invited to engage in an act of faith that education would elevate them morally, refine them culturally, and advance them socially. The readers took their cue from the cultural style of the Victorian middle class, which approached life with remarkable certitude. The means and ends of living were clear, and so the characteristic tone of the era—didactic, earnest, and moralistic—pervades the McGuffeys. That the McGuffey readers were hallmarks of middle-class Victorian culture is especially clear in the 1879 edition's treatment of men and women. In selections such as "True Courage" and "True Manliness" students were taught that bourgeois masculinity meant responsibility and duty above all; in "House-Cleaning," "The Greedy Girl," and "A Place for Every Thing," women's domestic roles were spelled out; and in "My Mother's Bible" and "Rock Me to Sleep," sentimental longings for maternal care were elevated to the highest of feelings.[56]

The McGuffey readers are fascinating historical documents, not

Cover of *McGuffey's Third Eclectic Reader,* 1879 edition.

because they represented perfect school texts, a platonic ideal to which America should return. As a way to teach reading, spelling, grammar, elocution and so forth, they were probably no worse than many textbooks of the era, maybe even a bit better than most. Memorization and recitation, the building blocks of nineteenth century pedagogy, were not peculiar to the McGuffeys, and what those techniques gave children by indoctrinating them with a body of knowledge, they took away with brain-numbing routine.

What makes the McGuffeys interesting today is not their inherent pedagogical value, but how their underlying tone of moral certitude and their modeling of rigid social roles helps us understand the ways that Victorian-era Americans viewed the world. As much as any single source can, the McGuffey readers offer us a window on nineteenth-century American culture by revealing some of the key ideological values, assumptions, and beliefs by which a particular segment of this society made sense of life.

Even in their golden age, the McGuffey readers were never simply a snapshot of nineteenth-century America. A better metaphor is to think of them as a map for building a national culture, one drawn by bourgeois Protestants who were white, largely descended from English and Western European stock, and who expected the country to be just like them. The readers' mantra of piety, conscience, and sober self-control helped socialize children into the ways of this Protestant middle class. Students who learned their lessons well and embraced the life offered them expected to enjoy the rewards promised.

Certainly by the early twentieth century, the readers no longer held sway as the dominant schoolbooks in the country. The reasons were varied: increasing religious and ethnic diversity came with a massive upsurge in immigration; large numbers of African Americans migrated to the North, making the country less homogeneous than ever; the burgeoning cities developed rhythms of work and leisure far different from McGuffey's bucolic ideal; the rise of a consumer culture blandished pleasures undreamed of in McGuffey's world; new methods of education transformed classrooms and schools into much larger, more complex places; and publishing businesses themselves expanded and diversified with the rest of the capitalist economy as new textbooks on a range of academic subjects flooded the market.

Still, the readers never completely lost their hold.

Henry Ford, one of America's great industrialists, who invented the assembly line, thereby revolutionizing automobile production, and who was also notoriously anti-Semitic and deeply suspicious of foreigners, looked with longing to the McGuffeys. So entranced was he with his memories of the readers that he had the 1857 edition (the one he read as a boy) reprinted. He gave away thousands of copies to friends and admirers, as well as to high school and college libraries. This early-twentieth-century captain of industry used to retreat to the nineteenth-century village he reconstructed in Greenfield, Michigan, where he would sit at a student desk in the one-room schoolhouse and read from the McGuffey texts, just as he had done as a child. Here, apparently, Ford found a moment of peace from the industrial world he had done so much to create.[57]

On June 15, 1941, thousands of men and women gathered in Oxford, Ohio, for the dedication of a McGuffey memorial, which stands today in front of Miami University's School of Education, housed in McGuffey Hall. Below a bronze casting are the words "William Holmes McGuffey, 1800–1873, who while professor in Miami University, compiled the famous McGuffey Readers which established the social standards of the great middle west of the United States for three quarters of a century." Dean Harvey C. Minnich raised the money to build the memorial, largely from the dozens of local McGuffey societies he helped to found throughout the region. It was the members of the McGuffey societies, mostly middle-aged and elderly people who gathered together regularly to read and recite from their old schoolbooks, who supported Minnich's efforts to create a McGuffey museum, acquire editions and translations of the readers, and collect the professor's correspondence and memorabilia.[58]

Just a decade later, the *New York Times Magazine* noted approvingly that President Harry S. Truman often praised the McGuffey readers to White House visitors for "educating for ethics as well as intellect, building character along with vocabulary." By the late twentieth century, *U.S. News and World Report* noted a mini revival of the readers, citing a figure of 150,000 copies sold in 1980. The magazine described how in Bristol, Virginia, children's reading abilities soared when they began studying with the McGuffeys, even though test results were not yet available to confirm this miracle. Some evangelical families still insist on using the readers today, especially the original edition, to educate their children.[59]

Even in the nineteenth century, at the height of their popularity, nostalgia for a mythic America that never really existed was part of the McGuffeys' appeal. We need to understand that nostalgia, not succumb to it, however. The great attorney of the early twentieth century, Clarence Darrow—socialist, defender of labor radicals, tribune of unpopular causes—helps us capture the ambiguous legacy of the McGuffey readers. The son of a large family of modest means, Darrow grew up in Kinsman, Ohio, in the 1860s and 1870s. He was raised on the readers. Tongue in cheek, he wonders aloud in his autobiography if there really was such a man as McGuffey. How could one person know so much and be so good? Did McGuffey have side whiskers, which were always a mark of distinction in Kinsman? Above all, Darrow recalls, the readers were full of advice on conduct and morals: "I am sure that no set of books ever came from any press that was so packed with love and righteousness as were those readers. Their religious and ethical stories seem silly now, but at the time it never occurred to me that those tales were utterly impossible lies which average children should easily have seen through." Righteousness and love on the one hand, lies to be seen through on the other. Certainly Darrow's mixed feelings of affection and estrangement, the sense that the McGuffeys expressed something important from his past that he had since outgrown, are a better way to understand the readers than the uncritical sentimentality that often surrounds them.[60]

NOTES

[1]Herbert Quick, *One Man's Life: An Autobiography* (Indianapolis: Bobbs-Merrill Company, 1925), 153–63.

[2]Ibid.

[3]Ibid.

[4]John H. Westerhoff, *McGuffey and His Readers* (Nashville: Abingdon Press, 1978), 14–17.

[5]Richard D. Mosier, *Making the American Mind: Social and Moral Ideas in the McGuffey Readers* (New York: Russell and Russell, 1965), 168–69.

[6]Ruth Miller Elson, *Guardians of Tradition: American Schoolbooks of the Nineteenth Century* (Lincoln: University of Nebraska Press, 1964), chs. 3, 5, 10. Elson is especially strong on the role of textbooks in American civil religion.

[7]Dolores P. Sullivan, *William Holmes McGuffey, Schoolmaster to the Nation* (Rutherford, N.J.: Fairleigh Dickinson University Press, 1994), 31–36.

[8]Ibid., 37–42.

[9]Ibid., 40–43.

[10]Ibid., 43–45.

[11]Andrew Wylie (Washington, Pa.) to William Holmes McGuffey, (Oxford, Ohio), February 6, 1826, in McGuffey's collected correspondence, Walter Havighurst Special Collections, King Library, Miami University, Oxford, Ohio.

[12]Sullivan, *William Holmes McGuffey,* 46–63. Also see Walter Havighurst, *The Miami Years: 1809–1984* (New York: Putnam, 1971), chs. 3, 4.

[13]Henry Wise, for example, suggested that McGuffey would best serve himself by becoming an attorney rather than a minister, and that there would be no contradiction between self-aggrandizement and service to God and country. Meanwhile, A. W. Wylie grew tired of the factionalism, back stabbing, and inuendo he found among the faculty in Washington, Pennsylvania. H. A. Wise (Winchester, Va.) to W. H. McGuffey (Oxford, Ohio), March 13, 1827; A. W. Wylie (Washington, Pa.) to W. H. McGuffey (Oxford, Ohio), April 25, 1828, both in McGuffey's collected correspondence, King Library, Miami University.

[14]See Andrew R. L. Cayton's excellent *The Frontier Republic: Ideology and Politics in the Ohio Country, 1780–1825* (Kent, Ohio: Kent State University Press, 1986), ch. 9.

[15]Andrew R. L. Cayton and Peter S. Onuf, *The Midwest and the Nation: Rethinking the History of an American Region* (Bloomington: Indiana University Press, 1990), 59–61; Wayne Urban and Jennings Wagoner Jr., *American Education: A History* (New York: McGraw Hill, 1996), 96–97.

[16]Publishers Truman and Smith were explicit about the importance of developing the region. The firm sought not only "to meet the wants of the West," but to provide an outlet for "Western talent and Western enterprise." Truman and Smith printed these claims on fly-leaf pages of the McGuffeys' first edition.

[17]McGuffey also apparently borrowed freely from other published collections, not an uncommon practice in an age when copyright laws were difficult to enforce. Indeed, in 1838 Richardson, Hart and Hobrook, publishers of the Worcester Readers, sued McGuffey and Truman and Smith for plagiarism. After a few editorial changes were made in subsequent editions, the suit was dropped. McGuffey's development of the readers and the plagiarism charges are best told in Westerhoff, *McGuffey and His Readers,* 17, 54–56.

[18]See the selection from the "Plea for the West," reprinted in this volume from the 1879 sixth reader under the title "Necessity of Education" (p. 99); Lawrence A. Cremin, *American Education, the National Experience, 1783–1876* (New York: Harper and Row, 1980), 36–39.

[19]The connections between Protestantism and capitalism were most provocatively articulated by the German sociologist Max Weber, but for a striking historical study, see Paul E. Johnson, *A Shopkeeper's Millennium: Society and Revivals in Rochester, New York, 1815–1837* (New York: Hill and Wang, 1978), ch. 6 and Afterword.

[20]This was roughly three times a common laborer's yearly salary in the 1830s, and it must have looked like a fortune to the professor; he took the cash, probably thinking he had made a good deal, for there was no reason to believe that his works eventually would sell so spectacularly.

[21]On the terms of McGuffey's contract, see Sullivan, *William Holmes McGuffey,* 58–59.

[22]Urban and Wagoner, *American Education,* 93–117; Carl F. Kaestle, *Pillars of the Republic: Common School and American Society, 1780–1860* (New York: Hill and Wang, 1983), 115–16, 128–35.

[23]James H. Rodabaugh, "Miami University, Calvinism, and the Anti-Slavery Movement" *Ohio State Archaeological and Historical Quarterly* 48(1) (January 1939): 66–73; transcript of paper on McGuffey by J. W. Scott, Miami faculty member, September 1, 1836, in the McGuffey Papers, King Library, Miami University. The most authoritative source on McGuffey's life up to his years at Miami is Westerhoff, *McGuffey and His Readers,* ch. 1; Also very useful, especially for the post-Miami years, is Sullivan, *William Holmes McGuffey,* chs. 4, 5.

[24]Sullivan, *William Holmes McGuffey,* chs. 4, 5.

[25]Westerhoff argues for a sharper break between the original edition and later ones than I believe is warranted. But he does make a compelling case for the evangelical foundations of the first readers. See Westerhoff, *McGuffey and His Readers,* 61–62.

[26]This argument has been made about various facets of American culture, but for a particularly clear expression of it, see Daniel T. Rodgers, *The Work Ethic in Industrial America: 1850–1920* (Chicago: University of Chicago Press, 1978), esp. ch. 4. For a more pithy example, see his "Socializing Middle-Class Children: Institutions, Fables, and Work Values in Nineteenth-Century America," in *Growing Up in America: Children in Historical Perspective,* ed. N. Ray Hines and Joseph M. Hawes (Urbana: University of Illinois Press, 1985).

[27]For two brilliant case studies on the interconnections between such social, religious, and economic change, see Paul E. Johnson, *Shopkeeper's Millenium,* and Mary P. Ryan, *Cradle of the Middle Class: The Family in Oneida County, New York, 1790–1865* (Cambridge: Cambridge University Press, 1981).

[28]Kaestle, *Pillars of the Republic,* ch. 8; David Thelen, *Paths of Resistance: Tradition and Dignity in Industrializing Missouri* (New York: Oxford University Press, 1986), 108–16.

[29]Ibid.; also see Catholic National Series: *New Fifth Reader* (New York: Benziger Bros., 1894), v–viii; Ray A. Billington, *The Protestant Crusade* (Gloucester, Mass.: Peter Smith, 1963); David Wallace Adams, *Education for Extinction: American Indians and the Boarding School Experience, 1875–1928* (Lawrence: University Press of Kansas, 1995), 136–63.

[30]See Urban and Wagoner, *American Education,* 111–113.

[31]These themes pervade the selections in this volume.

[32]For example, see "True Courage" from the 1879 third reader, reprinted on page 85.

[33]W. H. McGuffey (University of Virginia) to Charles McGuffey (Bremo Plantation), October 3, 1859, February 17, 1851, March 15, 1851, all in McGuffey's collected correspondence, King Library, Miami University.

[34]Harvey C. Minnich, *William Holmes McGuffey and His Readers* (New York: American Book Company, 1936), 54–57; Sullivan, *William Holmes McGuffey,* 26, 27; Elson, *Guardians of Tradition,* 7.

[35]Elson, *Guardians of Tradition,* ch. 4

[36]Ibid., 27–41

[37]Ibid., ch. 6. For an especially fine discussion on how schools were culturally contested ground between the middle class and those less privileged, see Thelen, *Paths of Resistance,* pp. 108–16.

[38]Elson, *Guardians of Tradition,* chs. 9, 10; Rodgers, "Socializing Middle-Class Children," 120–24.

[39]Ian Michael, *The Teaching of English: From the Sixteenth Century to 1870* (Cambridge: Cambridge University Press, 1987); Sullivan, *William Holmes McGuffey,* 23.

[40]Joseph Kett, *Rites of Passage: Adolescence in America, 1790 to the Present* (New York: Basic Books, 1977), 126–29, 152–54; Wayne E. Fuller, *One Room Schools of the Middle West: An Illustrated History* (Lawrence: University Press of Kansas, 1994), 46; Wayne E. Fuller, *The Old Country School: The Story of Rural Education in the Middle West* (Chicago: University of Chicago Press, 1982); E. Jennifer Monaghan and E. Wendy Saul, "The Reader, the Scribe, the Thinker: A Critical Look at Reading and Writing Instruction," in *The Formation of School Subjects,* ed. Thomas S. Popkewitz (New York: Falmer Press, 1987), 88–89; Cremin, *American Education,* 396. Also see William J. Reese, *The Origins of the American High School* (New Haven: Yale University Press, 1995).

[41]Cremin, *American Education,* 178–79; Kett, *Rites of Passage,* 126–29, 152–54, 158; Clarence Darrow, *The Story of My Life* (New York: Charles Scribner's and Sons, 1934) 18–21; Priscilla Ferguson Clement, "The City and the Child, 1860–1885," in *American Childhood: A Research Guide and Historical Handbook,* ed. Joseph M. Hawes and N. Ray Hiner (Westport: Greenwood Press, 1985), 245; Urban and Wagoner, *American Education,* 164–65, 170–77; Kaestle, *Pillars of the Republic,* 107–08. Kett points out that even by 1930, only about half of Americans in their midteens attended high school, while in 1920, just 8 percent of the population went to college. Still, the structure of a more specialized educational system—grammar school, high school, college—was in place just as the McGuffeys declined in popularity at the end of the nineteenth century. Clarence Darrow recalled in his autobiography that the sixth McGuffey reader was used in his high school, but generally, readers one through five were the property of the more democratic institution, the common school.

[42]Cremen, *American Education,* 180–81.

[43]Clement, "The City and the Child," 239–47; Barbara Finkelstein, "Casting Networks of Good Influence; the Reconstruction of Childhood in the United States, 1790–1870," in *American Childhood: A Research Guide and Historical Handbook,* ed. Hawes and Hiner, 124–30.

[44]Finkelstein, "Casting Networks," 130–35; Barbara Finkelstein, "Perfecting Childhood: Horace Mann and the Origins of Public Education in the United States," *Biography* 13(1) (Winter 1990): 12. On the social division of gender, Mary Ryan's *Cradle of the Middle Class* remains an outstanding work. Also see Urban and Wagoner, *American Education,* 114–16, 168–69; Kaestle, *Pillars of the Republic,* 122–26; Cremen, *American Education,* 398; Fuller,

The Old Country School, ch. 9; Elson, *Guardians of Tradition,* 300–22. The presence of boys and girls together in the schools is the subject of David Tyack and Elisabeth Hansot, *Learning Together: A History of Coeducation in American Public Schools* (New Haven: Yale University Press, 1990), esp. ch. 3.

[45]Urban and Wagoner, *American Education,* 114–16.

[46]Kaestle, *Pillars of the Republic,* 76–103.

[47]Lewis Atherton, *Main Street on the Middle Border* (Bloomington: Indiana University Press, 1954), 65–102.

[48]Points well-made by Atherton, in *Main Street,* ch. 3.

[49]The literature on the Great Strike of 1877 is extensive, but see Jeremy Brecher, *Strike!* (Boston: South End Press, 1977); Robert V. Bruce, *1877, Year of Violence* (Pathfinder, N.Y.: I. R. Dee, 1989); and Philip S. Foner, *The Great Labor Uprising of 1877* (New York: Monad Press, 1977).

[50]See especially Cayton and Onuf, *The Midwest and the Nation,* 52–55.

[51]Ibid., 55–59.

[52]Ibid., 59–64.

[53]Rodgers, "Socializing Middle-Class Children," 123. To survey the changes over time in the readers, see Stanley W. Lindberg, ed., *The Annotated McGuffey: Selections from the* McGuffey Eclectic Readers, *1836–1920* (New York: Van Nostrand Reinhold, 1976).

[54]Richard L. Bushman, *The Refinement of America: Persons, Houses, Cities* (New York: Knopf, 1992).

[55]Mosier recognizes that the McGuffeys were primarily an expression of Protestant, middle-class sensibilities, but having acknowledged this, he seems to equate hegemonic ideas with the entire culture.

[56]On Victorian culture, see, for example, Daniel Walker Howe, ed., *Victorian America* (Philadelphia: University of Pennsylvania Press, 1976).

[57]For a discussion by Ford of the McGuffeys, see *The Colophon,* n.s., 1(4) (Spring 1936): 587–88.

[58]See Hugh S. Fullerton, "That Guy McGuffey," *Saturday Evening Post,* November 26, 1927, 14; Hugh S. Fullerton, "Two Jolly Old Pedagogues," *Saturday Evening Post,* June 14, 1941, 27.

[59]Phyllis McGinley, "Lessons for Today: From McGuffey," *New York Times Magazine,* May 20, 1951, 9; Marvin Stone, "Ah, Good Old McGuffey," *U.S. News and World Report,* May 2, 1983, 76. In 1982, Mott Media Company began publishing a full series of the 1830s edition under the title "Original McGuffey Eclectic Series," which was designed especially for the marketplace in religious books. The series is still in print. Several pundits have suggested returning to the McGuffeys as a "solution" to contemporary school "problems." This position grows out of impossibly simplistic notions of a past golden age and equally fatuous preconceptions about education today. For an example, Sullivan's *William Holmes McGuffey* argues for a return to the McGuffeys with a remarkably dishonest and purile attack on how "liberals" have destroyed American education. See especially ch. 14.

[60]Darrow, *The Story of My Life,* 18–21.

PART TWO

Selections from the McGuffey Readers

1
Childhood

Most of the selections in this section are from *McGuffey's First Eclectic Reader.* Pedagogically, the great strength of these passages is that they are told from a child's point of view. In Lesson 51, for example, rather than have an omniscient narrator render judgement, the older boy explains in his own voice to the younger girl that God taught birds to make nests and that children should not disturb them. In addition, the lessons of the early readers are lavishly reinforced with engravings.

Texts and engravings depict childhood as a distinct stage of life—in McGuffey's time a relatively new idea in Western cultures—and education's task as protecting the innocence of children. This innocence, or lack of knowledge of evil, makes for an implicit connection between children and animals. In the following section, a mother hen rewards her chick's initiative, while squirrels offer friendship and wisdom to a kindly girl. For the Victorians, youth was the seedbed of character, the time when innocence might be strengthened or destroyed, so the selections took pains to impart moral ideals. The last lesson, which comes from the third reader, looks back on childhood with a nostalgic glow characteristic of the rest of the McGuffeys. In the lessons on childhood, how do the illustrations and the texts work together to shape beliefs?

Early Lessons

LESSON 22

Did you call us, mamma? I went with Tom to the pond. I had my doll, and Tom had his flag.

Lessons 22, 34, 37, 42, 55, 56, 62, 63, in *McGuffey's First Eclectic Reader,* ed. William Holmes McGuffey (New York: American Book Company, 1879), 27–28, 44–45, 49, 56–57, 78–79, 79–81, 91–92, 93–94. (Lessons in the first reader were numbered, not titled.)

The fat duck swam to the bank, and we fed her. Did you think we might fall into the pond?

We did not go too near, did we, Tom?

May we go to the swing, now, mamma?

LESSON 34

"Papa, may we have the big flag?", said James.

"What can my little boy do with such a big flag?"

"Hoist it on our tent, papa. We are playing Fourth of July."

"Is that what all this noise is about? Why not hoist your own flags?"

"Oh! they are too little."

"You might spoil my flag."

"Then we will all join to pay for it. But we will not spoil it, papa."

"Take it, then, and take the coil of rope with it."

"Oh! thank you. Hurrah for the flag, boys!"

LESSON 37

"What is that?" said Lucy, as she came out on the steps. "Oh, it is a little boat! What a pretty one it is!"

"I will give it to you when it is finished," said John, kindly. "Would you like to have it?"

"Yes, very much, thank you, John. Has grandma seen it?"

"Not yet; we will take it to her by and by. What have you in your pan, Lucy?"

"Some corn for my hens, John; they must be very hungry by this time."

LESSON 42

A little girl went in search of flowers for her mother. It was early in the day, and the grass was wet. Sweet little birds were singing all around her.

And what do you think she found besides flowers? A nest with young birds in it.

While she was looking at them, she heard the mother-bird chirp, as if she said, "Do not touch my children, little girl, for I love them dearly."

The little girl now thought how dearly her own mother loved her.

So she left the birds. Then, picking some flowers, she went home, and told her mother what she had seen and heard.

LESSON 55

"Come here, Rose. Look down into this bush."

"O Willie! a bird's nest! What cunning, little eggs! May we take it, and show it to mother?"

"What would the old bird do, Rose, if she should come back and not find her nest?"

"Oh, we would bring it right back, Willie!"

"Yes; but we could not fasten it in its place again. If the wind should blow it over, the eggs would get broken."

LESSON 56

"How does the bird make the nest so strong, Willie?"

"The mother-bird has her bill and her claws to work with, but she would not know how to make the nest if God did not teach her. Do you see what it is made of?"

"Yes, Willie, I see some horsehairs and some dry grass. The old bird must have worked hard to find all the hairs, and make them into such a pretty, round nest."

"Shall we take the nest, Rose?"

"Oh no, Willie! We must not take it; but we will come and look at it again, some time."

LESSON 62

"I never saw such children," said the old hen. "You don't try at all."

"We can't jump so far, mother. Indeed we can't, we can't!" chirped the little chickens.

"Well," said the old hen, "I must give it up." So she jumped back to the bank, and walked slowly home with her brood.

"I think mother asked too much of us," said one little chicken to the others.

"Well, I tried," said Chippy.

"We didn't," said the others; "it was of no use to try."

When they got home, the old hen began to look about for something to eat. She soon found, near the back door, a piece of bread.

So she called the chickens, and they all ran up to her, each one trying to get a bite at the piece of bread.

"No, no!" said the old hen. "This bread is for Chippy. He is the only one of my children that really tried to jump to the stone."

LESSON 63

We have come to the last lesson in this book. We have finished the First Reader.

You can now read all the lessons in it, and can write them on your slates.

Have you taken good care of your book? Children should always keep their books neat and clean.

Are you not glad to be ready for a new book?

Your parents are very kind to send you to school. If you are good, and if you try to learn, your teacher will love you, and you will please your parents.

Be kind to all, and do not waste your time in school.

When you go home, you may ask your parents to get you a Second Reader.

Patty and the Squirrel

1. Little Patty lives in a log house near a great forest. She has no sisters, and her big brothers are away all day helping their father.

2. But Patty is never lonely; for, though the nearest house is miles away, she has many little friends. Here are two of them that live in the woods.

3. But how did Patty teach them to be so tame? Patty came to the woods often, and was always so quiet and gentle that the squirrels soon found they need not be afraid of her.

4. She brought her bread and milk to eat under the trees, and was sure to leave crumbs for the squirrels.

5. When they came near, she sat very still and watched them. So, little by little, she made them her friends, till, at last, they would sit on her shoulder, and eat from her hand.

6. Squirrels build for themselves summer houses. These are made of leaves, and sticks, and moss. They are nice and cool for summer, but would never do for the winter cold and snow.

7. So these wise little people find a hollow in an old tree. They make it warm and snug with soft moss and leaves; and here the squirrels live all through the long winter.

"Patty and the Squirrel," Lesson 26, in *McGuffey's Second Eclectic Reader,* ed. William Holmes McGuffey (New York: American Book Company, 1879), 57–58.

Mamma's Present

1. Jessie played a good joke on her mamma. This is the way she did it.

2. Jessie had gone to the woods with Jamie and Joe to get green branches to trim up the house for Christmas. She wore her little cap, her white furs, and her red leggings.

3. She was a merry little girl, indeed; but she felt sad this morning because her mother had said, "The children will all have Christmas presents, but I don't expect any for myself. We are too poor this year."

4. When Jessie told her brothers this, they all talked about it a great deal. "Such a good, kind mamma, and no Christmas present! It's too bad."

5. "I don't like it," said little Jessie, with a tear in her eye.

6. "Oh, she has you," said Joe.

7. "But I am not something new," said Jessie.

8. "Well, you will be new, Jessie," said Joe, "when you get back. She has not seen you for an hour."

9. Jessie jumped and laughed. "Then put me in the basket, and carry me to mamma, and say, 'I am her Christmas present.' "

"Mamma's Present," Lesson 44, in *McGuffey's Second Eclectic Reader,* ed. William Holmes McGuffey (New York: American Book Company, 1879), 94–97.

10. So they set her in the basket, and put green branches all around her. It was a jolly ride. They set her down on the door-step, and went in and said, "There's a Christmas present out there for you, mamma."

11. Mamma went and looked, and there, in a basket of green branches, sat her own little laughing girl.

12. "Just the very thing I wanted most," said mamma.

13. "Then, dear mamma," said Jessie, bounding out of her leafy nest, "I should think it would be Christmas for mammas all the time, for they see their little girls every day."

Young Soldiers

1. Oh, were you ne'er a school-boy,
   And did you never train,
   And feel that swelling of the heart
   You ne'er can feel again?

2. Did you never meet, far down the street,
   With plumes and banners gay,
   While the kettle, for the kettle-drum,
   Played your march, march away?

3. It seems to me but yesterday,
   Nor scarce so long ago,
   Since all our school their muskets took,
   To charge the fearful foe.

4. Our muskets were of cedar wood,
   With ramrods bright and new;
   With bayonets forever set,
   And painted barrels, too.

5. We charged upon a flock of geese,
   And put them all to flight—
   Except one sturdy gander
   That thought to show us fight.

6. But, ah! we knew a thing or two;
   Our captain wheeled the van;

"Young Soldiers," Lesson 70, in *McGuffey's Third Eclectic Reader,* ed. William Holmes McGuffey (New York: American Book Company, 1879), 184–87.

We routed him, we scouted him,
  Nor lost a single man!

7. Our captain was as brave a lad
  As e'er commission bore;
And brightly shone his new tin sword;
  A paper cap he wore.

8. He led us up the steep hill-side,
  Against the western wind,
While the cockerel plume that decked his head
  Streamed bravely out behind.

9. We shouldered arms, we carried arms,
  We charged the bayonet;
And woe unto the mullen stalk
  That in our course we met!

10. At two o'clock the roll we called,
  And till the close of day,
With fearless hearts, though tired limbs,
  We fought the mimic fray,—
Till the supper-bell, from out the dell,
  Bade us march, march away.

2
Family

Home was a center of Victorian moral life. Ideally, men went into the world to earn a living in the market economy while women stayed home and attended to the moral and domestic needs of their families. Of course, women of poorer backgrounds labored as servants, in factories, or on farms, but the middle-class ideal depicted women as nurturers of the soul. It was believed that within the nuclear family children learned the values and men attained the security to civilize the outside world. The following selections emphasize the importance of family bonds, even as they differentiated family members into their roles by age and gender. But there was a strange melancholy here too. Despite the joyous reunion of mother and son in "The Lost Child," the story emphasizes how a mother's love for her children paled before God's love for sinners. Even more to the point, the last selection, "A Home Scene," contains much sadness and longing; here nostalgia was tinged with fear that family bonds could not withstand time and death. Do you consider these passages to be accurate depictions, or do they idealize nineteenth-century family life? On what evidence do you base your answer?

Evening at Home

1. It is winter. The cold wind whistles through the branches of the trees.

2. Mr. Brown has done his day's work, and his children, Harry and Kate, have come home from school. They learned their lessons well today, and both feel happy.

"Evening at Home," Lesson 1, in *McGuffey's Second Eclectic Reader,* ed. William Holmes McGuffey (New York: American Book Company, 1879), 11–12.

3. Tea is over. Mrs. Brown has put the little sitting-room in order. The fire burns brightly. One lamp gives light enough for all. On the stool is a basket of fine apples. They seem to say, "Won't you have one?"

4. Harry and Kate read a story in a new book. The father reads his newspaper, and the mother mends Harry's stockings.

5. By and by, they will tell one another what they have been reading about, and will have a chat over the events of the day.

6. Harry and Kate's bed-time will come first. I think I see them kiss their dear father and mother a sweet good-night.

7. Do you not wish that every boy and girl could have a home like this?

A Kind Brother

1. A boy was once sent from home to take a basket of things to his grandmother.

2. The basket was so full that it was very heavy. So his little brother went with him, to help carry the load.

3. They put a pole under the handle of the basket, and each then took hold of an end of the pole. In this way they could carry the basket very nicely.

4. Now the older boy thought, "My brother Tom does not know about this pole.

"A Kind Brother," Lesson 16, in *McGuffey's Second Eclectic Reader,* ed. William Holmes McGuffey (New York: American Book Company, 1879), 38–39.

5. "If I slip the basket near him, his side will be heavy, and mine light; but if the basket is in the middle of the pole, it will be as heavy for me as it is for him.

6. "Tom does not know this as I do. But I will not do it. It would be wrong, and I will not do what is wrong."

7. Then he slipped the basket quite near his own end of the pole. His load was now heavier than that of his little brother.

8. Yet he was happy; for he felt that he had done right. Had he deceived his brother, he would not have felt at all happy.

The Seven Sticks

1. A man had seven sons, who were always quarreling. They left their studies and work, to quarrel among themselves. Some bad men were looking forward to the death of their father, to cheat them out of their property by making them quarrel about it.

2. The good old man, one day, called his sons around him. He laid before them seven sticks, which were bound together. He said, "I will pay a hundred dollars to the one who can break this bundle."

3. Each one strained every nerve to break the bundle. After a long but vain trial, they all said that it could not be done.

4. "And yet, my boys," said the father, "nothing is easier to do." He then untied the bundle, and broke the sticks, one by one, with perfect ease.

5. "Ah!" said his sons, "it is easy enough to do it so; any body could do it in that way."

6. Their father replied, "As it is with these sticks, so is it with you, my sons. So long as you hold fast together and aid each other, you will prosper, and none can injure you.

7. "But if the bond of union be broken, it will happen to you just as it has to these sticks, which lie here broken on the ground."

Home, city, country, all are prosperous found,
When by the powerful link of union bound.

"The Seven Sticks," Lesson 44, in *McGuffey's Second Eclectic Reader,* ed. William Holmes McGuffey (New York: American Book Company, 1879), 115–17.

The Lost Child

1. A few years since, a child was lost in the woods. He was out with his brothers and sisters gathering berries, and was accidentally separated from them, and lost. The children, after looking in vain for some time in search of the little wanderer, returned, just in the dusk of the evening, to inform their parents that their brother was lost and could not be found.

2. The woods, at that time, were full of bears. The darkness of a cloudy night was rapidly coming on, and the alarmed father, gathering a few of his neighbors, hastened in search of the lost child. The mother remained at home, almost distracted with suspense.

3. As the clouds gathered, and the darkness increased, the father and the neighbors, with highly excited fears, traversed the woods in all directions, and raised loud shouts to attract the attention of the child. But their search was in vain. They could find no trace of the wanderer; and, as they stood under the boughs of the lofty trees, and listened, that if possible they might hear his feeble voice, no sound was borne to their ears but the melancholy moaning of the wind as it swept through the thick branches of the forest.

4. The gathering clouds threatened an approaching storm, and the deep darkness of the night had already enveloped them. It is difficult to conceive what were the feelings of that father. And who could imagine how deep the distress which filled the bosom of that mother, as she heard the wind, and beheld the darkness in which her child was wandering!

5. The search was continued in vain till nine o'clock in the evening. Then, one of the party was sent back to the village, to collect the inhabitants for a more extensive search. The bell rung the alarm, and the cry of fire resounded through the streets. It was ascertained, however, that it was not fire which caused the alarm, but that the bell tolled the more solemn tidings of a lost child.

6. Every heart sympathized in the sorrows of the distracted parents. Soon, multitudes of the people were seen ascending the hill, upon the declivity of which the village stood, to aid in the search. Ere long, the rain began to fall, but no tidings came back to the village of the lost child.

"The Lost Child," Lesson 61, in *McGuffey's Fourth Eclectic Reader,* ed. William Holmes McGuffey (New York: American Book Company, 1879), 165–68.

Hardly an eye was that night closed in sleep, and there was not a mother who did not feel for the parents.

7. The night passed away, and the morning dawned, and yet no tidings came. At last, those engaged in the search met together and held a consultation. They made arrangements for a more minute search, and agreed that, in case the child was found, a gun should be fired, to give a signal to the rest of the party.

8. As the sun arose, the clouds were scattered, and the whole landscape glittered in the rays of the bright morning. But that village was deserted and still. The stores were closed, and business was hushed. Mothers were walking the streets, with sympathizing countenances and anxious hearts. There was but one thought in every mind: "What has become of the lost child?"

9. All the affections and interest of the neighborhood were flowing in one deep and broad channel toward the little wanderer. About nine in the morning, the signal gun was fired, which announced that the child was found; and, for a moment, how dreadful was the suspense! Was it found a mangled corpse? or was it alive and well?

10. Soon, a joyful shout proclaimed the safety of the child. The shout was borne from tongue to tongue, till the whole forest rang again with the joyful sound. A messenger rapidly bore the tidings to the distracted mother. A procession was immediately formed by those engaged in the search. The child was placed upon a platform, hastily formed from the boughs of trees, and borne in triumph at the head of the procession. When they arrived at the brow of the hill, they rested for a moment, and proclaimed their success with three loud and animated cheers.

11. The procession then moved on till they arrived in front of the dwelling where the parents of the child resided. The mother, who stood at the door, with streaming eyes and throbbing heart, could no longer restrain herself or her feelings.

12. She rushed into the street, clasped her child to her bosom, and wept aloud. Every eye was filled with tears, and, for a moment, all were silent. But suddenly some one gave a signal for a shout. One loud, and long, and happy note of joy rose from the assembled multitude, and they went to their business and their homes.

13. There was more joy over the one child that was found than over the ninety and nine that went not astray. Likewise, there is joy in the presence of the angels of God over one sinner that repenteth. But still, this is a feeble representation of the love of our Father in heaven for us, and of the joy with which the angels welcome the returning wanderer.

14. The mother can not feel for her child that is lost as God feels for

the unhappy wanderer in the paths of sin. If a mother can feel so much, what must be the feelings of our Father in heaven for those who have strayed from his love? If man can feel so deep a sympathy, what must be the emotions which glow in the bosom of angels?

The Machinist's Return

1. On our way from Springfield to Boston, a stout, black-whiskered man sat immediately in front of me, in the drawing-room car, whose maneuvers were a source of constant amusement. He would get up every five minutes, hurry away to the narrow passage leading to the door of the car, and commence laughing in the most violent manner, continuing that healthful exercise until he observed that some one was watching him, when he would return to his seat.

2. As we neared Boston these demonstrations increased in frequency and violence, but the stranger kept his seat and chuckled to himself. He shifted the position of his two portmanteaus,[1] or placed them on the seat as if he was getting ready to leave. As we were at least twenty-five miles from Boston, such early preparations seemed extremely ridiculous. He became so excited at last that he could not keep his secret. Some one must be made a confidant; and as I happened to be the nearest to him, he selected me.

3. Turning around suddenly, and rocking himself to and fro in his chair, he said, "I have been away from home three years. Have been in Europe. My folks don't expect me for three months yet, but I got through and started. I telegraphed them at the last station—they've got the dispatch by this time." As he said this he rubbed his hands, and changed the portmanteau on his left to the right, and then the one on the right to the left.

4. "Have you a wife?" said I. "Yes, and three children," was the answer. He then got up and folded his overcoat anew, and hung it over the back of the seat. "You are somewhat nervous just now, are you not?" said I.

5. "Well, I should think so," he replied. "I haven't slept soundly for a week. Do you know," he went on, speaking in a low tone, "I am almost certain this train will run off the track and break my neck before I get to Boston. I have had too much good luck lately for one man. It can't last. It rains so hard, sometimes, that you think it's never going to stop; then

[1] Large suitcases.

"The Machinist's Return," Lesson 59, in *McGuffey's Fifth Eclectic Reader,* ed. William Holmes McGuffey (New York: American Book Company, 1879), 185–89.

it shines so bright you think it's always going to shine; and just as you are settled in either belief, you are knocked over by a change, to show you that you know nothing about it."

6. "Well, according to your philosophy," I said, "you will continue to have sunshine because you are expecting a storm." "Perhaps so," he replied; "but it is curious that the only thing which makes me think I shall get through safe is, I fear that I shall not."

7. "I am a machinist," he continued; "I made a discovery; nobody believed in it; I spent all my money in trying to bring it out; I mortgaged my home—every thing went. Every body laughed at me—every body but my wife. She said she would work her fingers off before I should give it up. I went to England. At first I met with no encouragement whatever, and came very near jumping off London bridge. I went into a workshop to earn money enough to come home with: there I met the man I wanted. To make a long story short, I've brought home £50,000 with me, and here I am."

8. "Good!" I exclaimed. "Yes," said he, "and the best of it is, she knows nothing about it. She has been disappointed so often that I concluded I would not write to her about my unexpected good luck. When I got my money, though, I started for home at once."

9. "And now, I suppose, you will make her happy?" "Happy!" he replied; "why, you don't know any thing about it! She's worked night and day since I have been in England, trying to support herself and the children decently. They paid her thirteen cents apiece for making shirts, and that's the way she has lived half the time. She'll come down to the depot to meet me in a gingham dress and a shawl a hundred years old, and she'll think she's dressed up! Perhaps she won't have any fine dresses in a week or so, eh?"

10. The stranger then strode down the passage-way again, and getting in a corner where he seemed to suppose that he was out of sight, went through the strangest pantomime,—laughing, putting his mouth into the drollest shapes, and swinging himself back and forth in the limited space.

11. As the train was going into the depot, I placed myself on the platform of the car in front of the one in which I had been riding, and opposite the stranger, who, with a portmanteau in each hand, was standing on the lowest step, ready to jump to the ground. I looked from his face to the faces of the people before us, but saw no sign of recognition. Suddenly he cried, "There they are!"

12. Then he laughed outright, but in a hysterical way, as he looked over the crowd in front of him. I followed his eye and saw, some distance back, as if crowded out by the well-dressed and elbowing throng, a little woman in a faded dress and a well-worn hat, with a face almost painful in its intense but hopeful expression, glancing rapidly from window to window as the coaches passed by.

13. She had not seen the stranger, but a moment after she caught his eye. In another instant he had jumped to the platform with his two portmanteaus, and, pushing his way through the crowd, he rushed towards the place where she was standing. I think I never saw a face assume so many different expressions in so short a time as did that of the little woman while her husband was on his way to meet her.

14. She was not pretty,—on the contrary, she was very plain-looking; but somehow I felt a big lump rise in my throat as I watched her. She was trying to laugh, but, God bless her, how completely she failed in the attempt! Her mouth got into the position to laugh, but it never moved after that, save to draw down at the corners and quiver, while her eyes blinked so fast that I suspect she only caught occasional glimpses of the broad-shouldered fellow who elbowed his way so rapidly toward her.

15. As he drew close and dropped the portmanteaus, she turned to one side and covered her face with her hands; and thus she was when the strong man gathered her up in his arms as if she were a child, and held her sobbing to his breast.

16. There were enough staring at them, heaven knows; so I turned my eyes away a moment, and then I saw two boys in threadbare roundabouts standing near, wiping their eyes on their sleeves, and bursting into tears anew at every fresh demonstration on the part of their mother. When I looked at the stranger again he had his hat drawn over his eyes; but his wife was looking up at him, and it seemed as if the pent-up tears of those weary months of waiting were streaming through her eyelids.

DONALD GRANT MITCHELL

A Home Scene

1. Little does the boy know, as the tide of years drifts by, floating him out insensibly from the harbor of his home, upon the great sea of life, —what joys, what opportunities, what affections, are slipping from him into the shades of that inexorable Past, where no man can go, save on the wings of his dreams.

2. Little does he think, as he leans upon the lap of his mother, with his

Donald Grant Mitchell, "A Home Scene," Lesson 97, in *McGuffey's Fifth Eclectic Reader,* ed. William Holmes McGuffey (New York: American Book Company, 1879), 292–95.

eye turned to her, in some earnest pleading for a fancied pleasure of the hour, or in some important story of his griefs, that such sharing of his sorrows, and such sympathy with his wishes, he will find nowhere again.

3. Little does he imagine that the fond sister Nelly, ever thoughtful of his pleasures, ever smiling away his griefs, will soon be beyond the reach of either; and that the waves of the years which come rocking so gently under him will soon toss her far away, upon the great swell of life.

4. But *now,* you are there. The fire-light glimmers upon the walls of your cherished home. The big chair of your father is drawn to its wonted corner by the chimney side; his head, just touched with gray, lies back upon its oaken top. Opposite sits your mother: her figure is thin, her look cheerful, yet subdued;—her arm perhaps resting on your shoulder, as she talks to you in tones of tender admonition, of the days that are to come.

5. The cat is purring on the hearth; the clock that ticked so plainly when Charlie died is ticking on the mantel still. The great table in the middle of the room, with its books and work, waits only for the lighting of the evening lamp, to see a return to its stores of embroidery and of story.

6. Upon a little stand under the mirror, which catches now and then a flicker of the fire-light, and makes it play, as if in wanton, upon the ceiling, lies that big book, reverenced of your New England parents—the Family Bible. It is a ponderous, square volume, with heavy silver clasps, that you have often pressed open for a look at its quaint, old pictures, or for a study of those prettily bordered pages, which lie between the Testaments, and which hold the Family Record.

7. There are the Births;—your father's and your mother's; it seems as if they were born a long time ago; and even your own date of birth appears an almost incredible distance back. Then, there are the Marriages;—only one as yet; and your mother's name looks oddly to you: it is hard to think of her as any one else than your doting parent.

8. Last of all came the Deaths;—only one. Poor Charlie! How it looks!—"Died, 12 September, 18—, Charles Henry, aged four years." You know just how it looks. You have turned to it often; there you seem to be joined to him, though only by the turning of a leaf.

9. And over your thoughts, as you look at that page of the Record, there sometimes wanders a vague, shadowy fear, which *will* come,—that your own name may soon be there. You try to drop the notion, as if it were not fairly your own; you affect to slight it, as you would slight a boy who presumed on your acquaintance, but whom you have no desire to know.

10. Yet your mother—how strange it is!—has no fears of such dark fancies. Even now, as you stand beside her, and as the twilight deepens

in the room, her low, silvery voice is stealing upon your ear, telling you that she can not be long with you;—that the time is coming, when you must be guided by your own judgment, and struggle with the world unaided by the friends of your boyhood.

11. There is a little pride, and a great deal more of anxiety, in your thoughts now, as you look steadfastly into the home-blaze, while those delicate fingers, so tender of your happiness, play with the locks upon your brow. To struggle with the world,—that is a proud thing; to struggle alone,—there lies the doubt! Then crowds in swift upon the calm of boyhood the first anxious thought of youth.

12. The hands of the old clock upon the mantel, that ticked off the hours when Charlie sighed, and when Charlie died, draw on toward midnight. The shadows that the fire-flame makes, grow dimmer and dimmer. And thus it is, that Home,—boy-home, passes away forever,—like the swaying of a pendulum,—like the fading of a shadow on the floor.

3
Virtues

Victorian moral earnestness was especially aimed at children because it was believed that during youth the habits and ideas of a lifetime were formed. Countless books and magazine articles advised children about everything from respect for their parents to studying hard in school. In the following selections, the McGuffeys teach some simple yet important values: orderliness, effort, contentment, cheerfulness toward others, and dependability. Such ideals had many sources and many applications; certainly kindness and empathy were Christian virtues. But many of these values also served the larger outside world in general and the market economy in particular. The virtues inculcated here made for reliable employees. They also helped secure social order, no small accomplishment because fear of disorder was ever present in an egalitarian democracy. In what sense were the virtues described here not merely personal characteristics but bulwarks of society?

A Place for Every Thing

Mary. I wish you would lend me your thimble, Sarah. I can never find my own.

Sarah. Why is it, Mary, you can never find it?

Mary. How can I tell? But if you will not lend me yours, I can borrow one elsewhere.

Sarah. I am willing to lend mine to you, Mary. But I would very much like to know why you come to me to borrow so often.

Mary. Because you never lose any of your things, and always know where to find them.

"A Place for Every Thing," Lesson 58, in *McGuffey's Second Eclectic Reader,* ed. William Holmes McGuffey (New York: American Book Company, 1879), 126–29.

Sarah. And why do I always know where to find my things?

Mary. I do not know why, I am sure. If I did know, I might sometimes find my own.

Sarah. I will tell you the secret. I have a place for every thing, and I put every thing in its place when I have done using it.

Mary. O Sarah! who wants to run and put away a thing as soon as she has used it, as if her life depended upon it?

Sarah. Our life does not depend upon it, but our comfort does, surely. How much more time will it take to put a thing in its place, than to hunt for it or to borrow whenever you want to use it?

Mary. Well, Sarah, I will never borrow of you again, you may depend upon it.

Sarah. You are not offended with me, I hope.

Mary. No, but I am ashamed. Before night, I will have a place for every thing, and then I will keep every thing in its place. You have taught me a lesson that I shall remember.

Jenny's Call

1. "It's of no use, Mrs. Templar; I have been trying the greater part of an hour to catch that rogue of a horse. She won't be caught."

2. Such was the report the hired man brought in to Mrs. Templar one pleasant May morning, when she had been planning a ride.

3. "I suppose it can not be helped, but I wanted her very much," she said, as she turned away.

4. "What was it you wanted, mother?" asked Jenny Templar, a bright, brown-haired, brown-eyed girl of twelve, who had just come into the room.

"Jenny's Call," Lesson 64, in *McGuffey's Second Eclectic Reader,* ed. William Holmes McGuffey (New York: American Book Company, 1879), 140–44.

5. "Fanny," said the mother. "It is such a beautiful morning, I meant to drive down to the village, get some groceries, then call for your Aunt Ann, have a nice ride up the river road, and bring her home to dinner.

6. "But father is away for all day, and the men have been trying nearly an hour to catch Fanny; one of the men says she can't be caught."

7. "Maybe she can't by him," said Jenny, with a merry laugh. "But, get ready, mother; you shall go if you like. I'll catch Fanny, and harness her, too."

8. "Why, my child, they say she jumped the ditch three or four times, and acted like a wild creature. You'll only be late at school, and tire yourself for nothing."

9. "It won't take me long, mother. Fanny will come to me," said Jenny, cheerily. She put on her wide straw hat, and was off in a moment, down the hill, to the field where the horse was grazing.

10. The moment Fanny heard the rustle of Jenny's dress, she pricked up her ears, snorted, and, with head erect, seemed ready to bound away again.

11. "Fanny! O Fanny!" called Jenny, and the beautiful creature turned her head. That gentle tone she well knew, and, glad to see her friend, she came directly to the fence, and rubbed her head on the girl's shoulder. As soon as the gate was opened, she followed Jenny to the barn.

12. The men had treated her roughly, and she remembered it. But she knew and loved the voice that was always kind, and the hand that often fed and caressed her. She gave love for love, and willing service for kindness.

MARIAN DOUGLAS

Cheerfulness

There is a little maiden –
Who is she? Do you know?
Who always has a welcome,
Wherever she may go.

Her face is like the May time,
Her voice is like a bird's;
The sweetest of all music
Is in her lightsome words.

Each spot she makes the brighter,
As if she were the sun;
And she is sought and cherished
And loved by every one;

By old folks and by children,
By lofty and by low:
Who is this little maiden?
Does any body know?

You surely must have met her;
You certainly can guess;
What! I must introduce her?
Her name is Cheerfulness.

Marian Douglas, "Cheerfulness," Lesson 70, in *McGuffey's Second Eclectic Reader,* ed. William Holmes McGuffey (New York: American Book Company, 1879), 158–59.

Lend a Hand

1. Lend a hand to one another
In the daily toil of life:
When we meet a weaker brother,
Let us help him in the strife.
There is none so rich but may,
In his turn, be forced to borrow;
And the poor man's lot to-day
May become our own to-morrow.

2. Lend a hand to one another:
When malicious tongues have thrown
Dark suspicion on your brother,
Be not prompt to cast a stone.
There is none so good but may
Run adrift in shame and sorrow;
And the good man of to-day
May become the bad to-morrow.

3. Lend a hand to one another:
In the race for Honor's crown;
Should it fall upon your brother,
Let not envy tear it down.
Lend a hand to all, we pray,
In their sunshine or their sorrow;
And the prize they've won to-day
May become our own to-morrow.

"Lend a Hand," Lesson 6, in *McGuffey's Third Eclectic Reader,* ed. William Holmes McGuffey (New York: American Book Company, 1879), 25–26.

When to Say No

1. Though "No" is a very little word, it is not always easy to say it; and the not doing so, often causes trouble.

2. When we are asked to stay away from school, and spend in idleness or mischief the time which ought to be spent in study, we should at once say "No."

3. When we are urged to loiter on our way to school, and thus be late, and interrupt our teacher and the school, we should say "No." When some school-mate wishes us to whisper or play in the school-room, we should say "No."

4. When we are tempted to use angry or wicked words, we should remember that the eye of God is always upon us, and should say "No."

5. When we have done any thing wrong, and are tempted to conceal it by falsehood, we should say "No, we can not tell a lie; it is wicked and cowardly."

6. If we are asked to do any thing which we know to be wrong, we should not fear to say "No."

7. If we thus learn to say "No," we shall avoid much trouble, and be always safe.

"When to Say No," Lesson 56, in *McGuffey's Third Eclectic Reader,* ed. William Holmes McGuffey (New York: American Book Company, 1879), 144–45.

The Contented Boy

Mr. Lenox was one morning riding by himself. He got off from his horse to look at something on the road-side. The horse broke away from him, and ran off. Mr. Lenox ran after him, but soon found that he could not catch him.

A little boy at work in a field near the road, heard the horse. As soon as he saw him running from his master, the boy ran very quickly to the middle of the road, and, catching the horse by the bridle, stopped him till Mr. Lenox came up.

"The Contented Boy," Lesson 60, in *McGuffey's Third Eclectic Reader,* ed. William Holmes McGuffey (New York: American Book Company, 1879), 151–55.

Mr. Lenox. Thank you, my good boy, you have caught my horse very nicely. What shall I give you for your trouble?

Boy. I want nothing, sir.

Mr. L. You want nothing? So much the better for you. Few men can say as much. But what were you doing in the field?

B. I was rooting up weeds, and tending the sheep that were feeding on turnips.

Mr. L. Do you like to work?

B. Yes, sir, very well, this fine weather.

Mr. L. But would you not rather play?

B. This is not hard work. It is almost as good as play.

Mr. L. Who set you to work?

B. My father, sir.

Mr. L. What is your name?

B. Peter Hurdle, sir.

Mr. L. How old are you?

B. Eight years old, next June.

Mr. L. How long have you been here?

B. Ever since six o'clock this morning.

Mr. L. Are you not hungry?

B. Yes, sir, but I shall go to dinner soon.

Mr. L. If you had a dime now, what would you do with it?

B. I don't know, sir. I never had so much.

Mr. L. Have you no playthings?

B. Playthings? What are they?

Mr. L. Such things as nine-pins, marbles, tops, and wooden horses.

B. No, sir. Tom and I play at foot-ball in winter, and I have a jumping-rope. I had a hoop, but it is broken.

Mr. L. Do you want nothing else?

B. I have hardly time to play with what I have. I have to drive the cows, and to run of errands, and to ride the horses to the fields, and that is as good as play.

Mr. L. You could get apples and cakes, if you had money, you know.

B. I can have apples at home. As for cake, I do not want that. My mother makes me a pie now and then, which is as good.

Mr. L. Would you not like a knife to cut sticks?

B. I have one. Here it is. Brother Tom gave it to me.

Mr. L. Your shoes are full of holes. Don't you want a new pair?

B. I have a better pair for Sundays.

Mr. L. But these let in water.

B. I do not mind that, sir.
Mr. L. Your hat is all torn, too.
B. I have a better one at home.
Mr. L. What do you do when it rains?
B. If it rains very hard when I am in the field, I get under a tree for shelter.
Mr. L. What do you do, if you are hungry before it is time to go home?
B. I sometimes eat a raw turnip.
Mr. L. But if there is none?
B. Then I do as well as I can without. I work on, and never think of it.
Mr. L. Why, my little fellow, I am glad to see that you are so contented. Were you ever at school?
B. No, sir. But father means to send me next winter.
Mr. L. You will want books then.
B. Yes, sir; each boy has a Spelling-book, a Reader, and a Testament.
Mr. L. Then I will give them to you. Tell your father so, and that it is because you are an obliging, contented little boy.
B. I will, sir. Thank you.
Mr. L. Good by, Peter.
B. Good morning, sir.

Try, Try Again

1. 'Tis a lesson you should heed,
   Try, try again;
   If at first you don't succeed,
   Try, try again;
   Then your courage should appear,
   For, if you will persevere,
   You will conquer, never fear;
   Try, try again.

2. Once or twice though you should fail,
   Try, try again;

"Try, Try Again," Lesson 2, in *McGuffey's Fourth Eclectic Reader,* ed. William Holmes McGuffey (New York: American Book Company, 1879), 28–29.

If you would at last prevail,
Try, try again;
If we strive, 'tis no disgrace
Though we do not win the race;
What should you do in the case?
Try, try again.

3. If you find your task is hard,
Try, try again;
Time will bring you your reward,
Try, try again.
All that other folks can do,
Why, with patience, should not you?
Only keep this rule in view:
Try, try again.

4

Vices

Victorian virtues and vices defined each other. As the first selection, "Pretty Is that Pretty Does," makes clear, appearances can deceive. In fact, one of the great fears in nineteenth-century democratic society was that certain individuals, like the murderous spider working hard in her plain brown dress, might manipulate the image of virtue. An open society that depended on individual self-control meant that each person must police not only his or her own behavior, but also keep watch on the neighbors. The readings in this section urge that gluttony, disobedience to authority, drunkenness, sloth, insolence, and greed be uncovered and stopped. Not only were they Christian sins, they had no place in a bourgeois society that prided itself on productivity and individual self-control. "The Festal Board," for example, warns how beguiling the life of passion and pleasure can be and how even small deviations from the straight and narrow lead to ruin. The final selection, "Taking Comfort," by John Greenleaf Whittier, plays on a popular literary convention of McGuffey's day that contrasted innocent nature with sinful men, not merely to berate the latter but to call them back to their better selves. Do you think that children were persuaded by these lessons?

ALICE CARY

Pretty Is that Pretty Does

1. The spider wears a plain brown dress,
   And she is a steady spinner;
   To see her, quiet as a mouse,
   Going about her silver house,

Alice Cary, "Pretty Is that Pretty Does," Lesson 49, in *McGuffey's Second Eclectic Reader,* ed. William Holmes McGuffey (New York: American Book Company, 1879), 107–08.

You would never, never, never guess
The way she gets her dinner.

2. She looks as if no thought of ill
In all her life had stirred her;
But while she moves with careful tread,
And while she spins her silken thread,
She is planning, planning, planning still
The way to do some murder.

3. My child, who reads this simple lay,
With eyes down-dropt and tender,
Remember the old proverb says
That pretty is which pretty does,
And that worth does not go nor stay
For poverty nor splendor.

4. 'Tis not the house, and not the dress,
That makes the saint or sinner.
To see the spider sit and spin,
Shut with her walls of silver in,
You would never, never, never guess
The way she gets her dinner.

The Greedy Girl

1. Laura English is a greedy little girl. Indeed, she is quite a glutton. Do you know what a glutton is? A glutton is one who eats too much, because the food tastes well.

2. Laura's mother is always willing she should have as much to eat as is good for her; but sometimes, when her mother is not watching, she eats so much that it makes her sick.

3. I do not know why she is so silly. Her kitten never eats more than it needs. It leaves the nice bones on the plate, and lies down to sleep when it has eaten enough.

4. The bee is wiser than Laura. It flies all day among the flowers to

"The Greedy Girl," Lesson 57, in *McGuffey's Second Eclectic Reader,* ed. William Holmes McGuffey (New York: American Book Company, 1879), 124–25.

gather honey, and might eat the whole time if it pleased. But it eats just enough, and carries all the rest to its hive.

5. The squirrel eats a few nuts or acorns, and frisks about as gayly as if he had dined at the king's table.

6. Did you ever see a squirrel with a nut in his paws? How bright and lively he looks as he eats it!

Harry and Annie

1. Harry and Annie lived a mile from town, but they went there to school every day. It was a pleasant walk down the lane, and through the meadow by the pond.

2. I hardly know whether they liked it better in summer or in winter. They used to pretend that they were travelers exploring a new country, and would scatter leaves on the road that they might find their way back again.

3. When the ice was thick and firm, they went across the pond. But their mother did not like to have them do this unless some one was with them.

4. "Don't go across the pond to-day, children," she said, as she kissed them and bade them good-bye one morning; "it is beginning to thaw."

5. "All right, mother," said Harry, not very good-naturedly, for he was very fond of running and sliding on the ice. When they came to the pond, the ice looked hard and safe.

6. "There," said he to his sister, "I knew it hadn't thawed any. Mother is always afraid we shall be drowned. Come along, we will have a good time sliding. The school bell will not ring for an hour at least."

7. "But you promised mother," said Annie.

8. "No, I didn't. I only said 'All right,' and it *is* all right."

9. "I didn't say any thing; so I can do as I like," said Annie.

10. So they stepped on the ice, and started to go across the pond. They had not gone far before the ice gave way, and they fell into the water.

11. A man who was at work near the shore, heard the screams of the children, and plunged into the water to save them. Harry managed to get

"Harry and Annie," Lesson 15, in *McGuffey's Third Eclectic Reader,* ed. William Holmes McGuffey (New York: American Book Company, 1879), 46–48.

to the shore without any help, but poor Annie was nearly drowned before the man could reach her.

12. Harry went home almost frozen, and told his mother how disobedient he had been. He remembered the lesson learned that day as long as he lived.

Beware of the First Drink

1. "Uncle Philip, as the day is fine, will you take a walk with us this morning?"

2. "Yes, boys. Let me get my hat and cane, and we will take a ramble. I will tell you a story as we go. Do you know poor old Tom Smith?"

3. "Know him! Why, Uncle Philip, every body knows him. He is such a shocking drunkard, and swears so horribly."

"Beware of the First Drink," Lesson 42, in *McGuffey's Third Eclectic Reader,* ed. William Holmes McGuffey (New York: American Book Company, 1879), 111–13.

4. "Well, I have known him ever since we were boys together. There was not a more decent, well-behaved boy among us. After he left school, his father died, and he was put into a store in the city. There, he fell into bad company.

5. "Instead of spending his evenings in reading, he would go to the theater and to balls. He soon learned to play cards, and of course to play for money. He lost more than he could pay.

6. "He wrote to his poor mother, and told her his losses. She sent him money to pay his debts, and told him to come home.

7. "He did come home. After all, he might still have been useful and happy, for his friends were willing to forgive the past. For a time, things went on well. He married a lovely woman, gave up his bad habits, and was doing well.

8. "But one thing, boys, ruined him forever. In the city, he had learned to take strong drink, and he said to me once, that when a man begins to drink, he never knows where it will end. 'Therefore,' said Tom, 'beware of the first drink!'

9. "It was not long before he began to follow his old habit. He knew the danger, but it seemed as if he could not resist his desire to drink. His poor mother soon died of grief and shame. His lovely wife followed her to the grave.

10. "He lost the respect of all, went on from bad to worse, and has long been a perfect sot. Last night, I had a letter from the city, stating that Tom Smith has been found guilty of stealing, and sent to the state-prison for ten years.

11. "There I suppose he will die, for he is now old. It is dreadful to think to what an end he has come. I could not but think, as I read the letter, of what he said to me years ago, 'Beware of the first drink!'

12. "Ah, my dear boys, when old Uncle Philip is gone, remember that he told you the story of Tom Smith, and said to you, 'Beware of the first drink!' The man who does this will never be a drunkard."

The Alarm-Watch

1. A lady, who found it not easy to wake in the morning as early as she wished, bought an alarm-watch. These watches are so made as to strike with a loud whirring noise, at any hour the owner pleases to set them.

2. The lady placed her watch at the head of the bed, and at the right time she found herself roused by the long, rattling sound.

3. She arose at once, and felt better all day for her early rising. This lasted for some weeks. The alarm-watch faithfully did its duty, and was plainly heard so long as it was obeyed.

4. But, after a time, the lady grew tired of early rising. When she was waked by the noise, she merely turned over in bed, and slept again.

5. In a few days, the watch ceased to rouse her from her sleep. It spoke just as loudly as ever; but she did not hear it, because she had been in the habit of not obeying it.

6. Finding that she might as well be without it, she resolved that when she heard the sound she would jump up.

7. Just so it is with conscience. If we will obey its voice, even in the most trifling things, we can always hear it, clear and strong.

"The Alarm-Watch," Lesson 50, in *McGuffey's Third Eclectic Reader,* ed. William Holmes McGuffey (New York: American Book Company, 1879), 130–32.

8. But if we allow ourselves to do what we have some fears may not be quite right, we shall grow more and more sleepy, until the voice of conscience has no longer power to wake us.

The Insolent Boy

1. James Selton was one of the most insolent boys in the village where he lived. He would rarely pass people in the street without being guilty of some sort of abuse.

2. If a person were well dressed he would cry out, "Dandy!" If a person's clothes were dirty or torn, he would throw stones at him, and annoy him in every way.

3. One afternoon, just as the school was dismissed, a stranger passed through the village. His dress was plain and somewhat old, but neat and clean. He carried a cane in his hand, on the end of which was a bundle, and he wore a broad-brimmed hat.

4. No sooner did James see the stranger, than he winked to his playmates, and said, "Now for some fun!" He then silently went toward the stranger from behind, and, knocking off his hat, ran away.

5. The man turned and saw him, but James was out of hearing before he could speak. The stranger put on his hat, and went on his way. Again did James approach; but this time, the man caught him by the arm, and held him fast.

6. However, he contented himself with looking James a moment in the face, and then pushed him from him. No sooner did the naughty boy find himself free again, than he began to pelt the stranger with dirt and stones.

7. But he was much frightened when the "rowdy," as he foolishly called the man, was struck on the head by a brick, and badly hurt. All the boys now ran away, and James skulked across the fields to his home.

8. As he drew near the house, his sister Caroline came out to meet him, holding up a beautiful gold chain and some new books for him to see.

9. She told James, as fast as she could talk, that their uncle, who had been away several years, had come home, and was now in the house; that he had brought beautiful presents for the whole family; that he had left

"The Insolent Boy," Lesson 62, in *McGuffey's Third Eclectic Reader,* ed. William Holmes McGuffey (New York: American Book Company, 1879), 158–62.

his carriage at the tavern, a mile or two off, and walked on foot, so as to surprise his brother, their father.

10. She said, that while he was coming through the village, some wicked boys threw stones at him, and hit him just over the eye, and that mother had bound up the wound. "But what makes you look so pale?" asked Caroline, changing her tone.

11. The guilty boy told her that nothing was the matter with him; and running into the house, he went up stairs into his chamber. Soon after, he heard his father calling him to come down. Trembling from head to foot, he obeyed. When he reached the parlor door, he stood, fearing to enter.

12. His mother said, "James, why do you not come in? You are not usually so bashful. See this beautiful watch, which your uncle has brought for you."

13. What a sense of shame did James now feel! Little Caroline seized his arm, and pulled him into the room. But he hung down his head, and covered his face with his hands.

14. His uncle went up to him, and kindly taking away his hands, said, "James, will you not bid me welcome?" But quickly starting back, he cried, "Brother, this is not your son. It is the boy who so shamefully insulted me in the street!"

15. With surprise and grief did the good father and mother learn this. His uncle was ready to forgive him, and forget the injury. But his father would never permit James to have the gold watch, nor the beautiful books, which his uncle had brought for him.

16. The rest of the children were loaded with presents. James was obliged to content himself with seeing them happy. He never forgot this lesson so long as he lived. It cured him entirely of his low and insolent manners.

The Festal Board

1. Come to the festal board to-night,
   For bright-eyed beauty will be there,
Her coral lips in nectar steeped,
   And garlanded her hair.

"The Festal Board," Lesson 18, in *McGuffey's Fifth Eclectic Reader,* ed. William Holmes McGuffey (New York: American Book Company, 1879), 78–80.

2. Come to the festal board to-night,
   For there the joyous laugh of youth
Will ring those silvery peals, which speak
   Of bosoms pure and stainless truth.

3. Come to the festal board to-night,
   For friendship, there, with stronger chain,
Devoted hearts already bound
   For good or ill, will bind again.
   I went.

4. Nature and art their stores outpoured
   Joy beamed in every kindling glance;
Love, friendship, youth, and beauty smiled;
   What could that evening's bliss enhance?
   We parted.

5. And years have flown; but where are now
   The guests, who round that table met?
Rises their sun as gloriously
   As on the banquet's eve it set?

6. How holds the chain which friendship wove?
   It broke; and soon the hearts it bound
Were widely sundered; and for peace,
   Envy, and strife, and blood were found.

7. The merriest laugh which then was heard,
   Has changed its tones to maniac screams,
As half-quenched memory kindles up
   Glimmerings of guilt in feverish dreams.

8. And where is she, whose diamond eyes
   Golconda's purest gems outshone?
Whose roseate lips of Eden breathed?
   Say, where is she, the beauteous one?

9. Beneath yon willow's drooping shade,
   With eyes now dim, and lips all pale,
She sleeps in peace. Read on her urn,
   "A broken heart." This tells her tale.

10. And where is he, that tower of strength,
   Whose fate with hers for life was joined?

How beats his heart, once honor's throne?
How high has soared his daring mind?

11. Go to the dungeon's gloom to-night;
His wasted form, his aching head,
And all that now remains of him,
Lies, shuddering, on a felon's bed.

12. Ask you of all these woes the cause?
The festal board, the enticing bowl,
More often came, and reason fled,
And maddened passions spurned control.

13. Learn wisdom, then. The frequent feast
Avoid; for there, with stealthy tread
Temptation walks, to lure you on,
Till death, at last, the banquet spread.

14. And shun, oh shun, the enchanted cup!
Though, now, its draught like joy appears,
Ere long it will be fanned by sighs,
And sadly mixed with blood and tears.

JOHN GREENLEAF WHITTIER

Taking Comfort

1. For the last few days, the fine weather has led me away from books and papers, and the close air of dwellings, into the open fields, and under the soft, warm sunshine, and the softer light of a full moon. The loveliest season of the whole year—that transient but delightful interval between the storms of the "wild equinox, with all their wet," and the dark, short, dismal days which precede the rigor of winter—is now with us. The sun rises through a soft and hazy atmosphere; the light mist-clouds melt gradually before him; and his noon-tide light rests warm and clear on still woods, tranquil waters, and grasses green with the late autumnal rains.

John Greenleaf Whittier, "Taking Comfort," Lesson 82, in *McGuffey's Fifth Eclectic Reader*, ed. William Holmes McGuffey (New York: American Book Company, 1879), 259–61.

2. One fine morning, not long ago, I strolled down the Merrimac, on the Tewksbury shore. I know of no walk in the vicinity of Lowell so inviting as that along the margin of the river, for nearly a mile from the village of Belvidere. The path winds, green and flower-skirted, among beeches and oaks, through whose boughs you catch glimpses of waters sparkling and dashing below. Rocks, huge and picturesque, jut out into the stream, affording beautiful views of the river and the distant city.

3. Half fatigued with my walk, I threw myself down upon a rocky slope of the bank, where the panorama of earth, sky, and water lay clear and distinct about me. Far above, silent and dim as a picture, was the city, with its huge mill-masonry, confused chimney-tops, and churchspires; near it rose the height of Belvidere, with its deserted burial-place and neglected grave-stones sharply defined on its bleak, bare summit against the sky; before me the river went dashing down its rugged channel, sending up its everlasting murmur; above me the birch-tree hung its tassels; and the last wild flowers of autumn profusely fringed the rocky rim of the water.

4. Right opposite, the Dracut woods stretched upwards from the shore, beautiful with the hues of frost, glowing with tints richer and deeper than those which Claude or Poussin mingled, as if the rainbows of a summer shower had fallen among them. At a little distance to the right, a group of cattle stood mid-leg deep in the river; and a troop of children, bright-eyed and mirthful, were casting pebbles at them from a projecting shelf of rock. Over all a warm but softened sunshine melted down from a slumberous autumnal sky.

5. My revery was disagreeably broken. A low, grunting sound, half bestial, half human, attracted my attention. I was not alone. Close beside me, half hidden by a tuft of bushes, lay a human being, stretched out at full length, with his face literally rooted into the gravel. A little boy, five or six years of age, clean and healthful, with his fair brown locks and blue eyes, stood on the bank above, gazing down upon him with an expression of childhood's simple and unaffected pity.

6. "What ails you?" asked the boy at length. "What makes you lie there?"

The prostrate groveler struggled half-way up, exhibiting the bloated and filthy countenance of a drunkard. He made two or three efforts to get upon his feet, lost his balance, and tumbled forward upon his face.

"What are you doing there?" inquired the boy.

"I'm taking comfort," he muttered, with his mouth in the dirt.

7. Taking his comfort! There he lay,—squalid and loathsome under

the bright heaven,—an imbruted man. The holy harmonies of Nature, the sounds of gushing waters, the rustle of the leaves above him, the wild flowers, the frost-bloom of the woods,—what were they to him? Insensible, deaf, and blind, in the stupor of a living death, he lay there, literally realizing that most bitterly significant Eastern malediction, *"May you eat dirt."*

5
Character

The goal of Victorian education, home life, and religious training was the building up of good character. The following selections present a drama for both their protagonists and their readers. A moment of decision is reached; one walks either the right path or the wrong one. Choosing honesty, charity, respect for elders, and so forth are all more costly and less fun than their alternatives, yet in each of these examples, children take the moral course. The lessons here not only taught particular values, they also imparted a sense of responsibility for others in a society that otherwise encouraged people to seize their opportunities. True courage consisted of listening to the voice of conscience, not to the blandishments or flatteries of others. Just in case children failed to get the message that virtue was its own reward, many of these stories end with the righteous path and the profitable one being the same. Certainly most Victorians would have argued that upright Christian behavior and good business complemented each other. Nonetheless, by the last two decades of the nineteenth century, amidst booming cities, labor unrest, and enormous concentrations of economic wealth, these lessons in individual character already had an archaic ring to them. Judging from these passages, which were the most dangerous character flaws? Why?

The Broken Window

1. George Ellet had a bright silver dollar for a New-year's gift.
2. He thought of all the fine things he might buy with it.
3. The ground was all covered with snow; but the sun shone out bright, and every thing looked beautiful.

"The Broken Window," Lesson 60, in *McGuffey's Second Eclectic Reader,* ed. William Holmes McGuffey (New York: American Book Company, 1879), 131–33.

4. So George put on his hat, and ran into the street. As he went skipping along, he met some boys throwing snow-balls. George soon engaged in the sport.

5. He sent a ball at James Mason, but it missed him, and broke a window on the other side of the street.

6. George feared some one would come out of the house and find him. So he ran off as fast as he could.

7. As soon as he got round the next corner, George stopped, because he was very sorry for what he had done.

8. He said to himself, "I have no right to spend my silver dollar, now. I ought to go back, and pay for the glass I broke with my snow-ball."

9. He went up and down the street, and felt very sad. He wished very much to buy something nice. He also wished to pay for the broken glass.

10. At last he said, "It was wrong to break the window, though I did not mean to do it. I will go and pay for it, if it takes all my money. I will try not to be sorry. I do not think the man will hurt me if I pay for the mischief I have done."

The Broken Window

(Concluded)

1. George started off, and felt much happier for having made up his mind to do what was right.

2. He rang the door-bell. When the man came out, George said, "Sir, I threw a snow-ball through your window. But I did not intend to do it. I am very sorry, and wish to pay you. Here is the dollar my father gave me as a New-year's gift."

3. The gentleman took the dollar, and asked George if he had no more money. George said he had not. "Well," said he, "this will do."

4. So, after asking George his name, and where he lived, he called him an honest boy, and shut the door.

5. George went home at dinner time, with a face as rosy, and eyes as

"The Broken Window (Concluded)", Lesson 61, in *McGuffey's Second Eclectic Reader,* ed. William Holmes McGuffey (New York: American Book Company, 1879), 133–35.

bright, as if nothing had gone wrong. At dinner, Mr. Ellet asked him what he had bought with his money.

6. George very honestly told him all about the broken window, and said he felt very well without any money to spend.

7. When dinner was over, Mr. Ellet told George to go and look in his cap. He did so, and found two silver dollars there.

8. The man, whose window had been broken, had been there, and told Mr. Ellet about it. He gave back George's dollar and another besides.

9. A short time after this, the man came and told Mr. Ellet that he wanted a good boy to stay in his store.

10. As soon as George left school, he went to live with this man, who was a rich merchant. In a few years he became the merchant's partner.

The New-Year

1. One pleasant New-year's morning, Edward rose, and washed and dressed himself in haste. He wanted to be first to wish a happy New-year.

2. He looked in every room, and shouted the words of welcome. He ran into the street, to repeat them to those he might meet.

3. When he came back, his father gave him two bright, new silver dollars.

4. His face lighted up as he took them. He had wished for a long time to buy some pretty books that he had seen at the book-store.

5. He left the house with a light heart, intending to buy the books.

6. As he ran down the street, he saw a poor German family, the father, mother, and three children shivering with cold.

7. "I wish you a happy New-year," said Edward, as he was gayly passing on. The man shook his head.

8. "You do not belong to this country," said Edward. The man again shook his head, for he could not understand or speak our language.

9. But he pointed to his mouth, and to the children, as if to say, "These little ones have had nothing to eat for a long time."

"The New-Year," Lesson 27, in *McGuffey's Third Eclectic Reader,* ed. William Holmes McGuffey (New York: American Book Company, 1879), 69–72.

10. Edward quickly understood that these poor people were in distress. He took out his dollars, and gave one to the man, and the other to his wife.

11. How their eyes sparkled with gratitude! They said something in their language, which doubtless meant, "We thank you a thousand times, and will remember you in our prayers."

12. When Edward came home, his father asked what books he had bought. He hung his head a moment, but quickly looked up.

13. "I have bought no books," said he, "I gave my money to some poor people, who seemed to be very hungry and wretched.

14. "I think I can wait for my books till next New-year. Oh, if you had seen how glad they were to receive the money!"

15. "My dear boy," said his father, "here is a whole bundle of books. I give them to you, more as a reward for your goodness of heart than as a New-year's gift.

16. "I saw you give the money to the poor German family. It was no small sum for a little boy to give cheerfully.

17. "Be thus ever ready to help the poor, and wretched, and distressed; and every year of your life will be to you a happy New-year."

True Courage

One cold winter's day, three boys were passing by a school-house. The oldest was a bad boy, always in trouble himself, and trying to get others into trouble. The youngest, whose name was George, was a very good boy.

George wished to do right, but was very much wanting in courage. The other boys were named Henry and James. As they walked along, they talked as follows:

Henry. What fun it would be to throw a snow-ball against the school-room door, and make the teacher and scholars all jump!

James. You would jump, if you should. If the teacher did not catch you and whip you, he would tell your father, and you would get a whipping then; and that would make you jump higher than the scholars, I think.

Henry. Why, we would get so far off, before the teacher could come to the door, that he could not tell who we are. Here is a snow-ball just as hard as ice, and George would as soon throw it against the door as not.

James. Give it to him, and see. He would not dare to throw it.

Henry. Do you think George is a coward? You do not know him as well as I do. Here, George, take this snow-ball, and show James that you are not such a coward as he thinks you are.

George. I am not afraid to throw it; but I do not want to. I do not see that it will do any good, or that there will be any fun in it.

James. There! I told you he would not dare to throw it.

Henry. Why, George, are you turning coward? I thought you did not fear any thing. Come, save your credit, and throw it. I know you are not afraid.

George. Well, I am not afraid to throw. Give me the snow-ball. I would as soon throw it as not.

Whack! went the snow-ball against the door; and the boys took to

"True Courage," Lesson 52, in *McGuffey's Third Eclectic Reader,* ed. William Holmes McGuffey (New York: American Book Company, 1879), 134–37.

their heels. Henry was laughing as heartily as he could, to think what a fool he had made of George.

George had a whipping for his folly, as he ought to have had. He was such a coward, that he was afraid of being called a coward. He did not dare refuse to do as Henry told him, for fear that he would be laughed at.

If he had been really a brave boy, he would have said, "Henry, do you suppose that I am so foolish as to throw that snow-ball, just because you want to have me? You may throw your own snow-balls, if you please!"

Henry would, perhaps, have laughed at him, and called him a coward.

But George would have said, "Do you think that I care for your laughing? I do not think it right to throw the snow-ball. I will not do that which I think to be wrong, if the whole town should join with you in laughing."

This would have been real courage. Henry would have seen, at once, that it would do no good to laugh at a boy who had so bold a heart. You must have this fearless spirit, or you will get into trouble, and will be, and ought to be, disliked by all.

Mary's Dime

1. There! I have drawn the chairs into the right corners, and dusted the room nicely. How cold papa and mamma will be when they return from their long ride! It is not time to toast the bread yet, and I am tired of reading.

2. What shall I do? Somehow, I can't help thinking about the pale face of that little beggar-girl all the time. I can see the glad light filling her eyes, just as plain as I did when I laid the dime in her little dirty hand.

3. How much I had thought of that dime, too! Grandpa gave it to me a whole month ago, and I had kept it ever since in my red box up-stairs;

"Mary's Dime," Lesson 64, in *McGuffey's Third Eclectic Reader,* ed. William Holmes McGuffey (New York: American Book Company, 1879), 167–69.

but those sugar apples looked so beautiful, and were so cheap—only a dime apiece—that I made up my mind to have one.

4. I can see her—the beggar-girl, I mean—as she stood there in front of the store, in her old hood and faded dress, looking at the candies laid all in a row. I wonder what made me say, "Little girl, what do you want?"

5. How she stared at me, just as if nobody had spoken kindly to her before. I guess she thought I was sorry for her, for she said, so earnestly and sorrowfully, "I was thinking how good one of those gingerbread rolls would taste. I haven't had any thing to eat to-day."

6. Now, I thought to myself, "Mary Williams, you have had a good breakfast and a good dinner this day, and this poor girl has not had a mouthful. You can give her your dime; she needs it a great deal more than you do."

7. I could not resist that little girl's sorrowful, hungry look—so I dropped the dime right into her hand, and, without waiting for her to speak, walked straight away. I'm so glad I gave her the dime, if I did have to go without the apple lying there in the window, and looking just like a real one.

No Crown for Me

1. "Will you come with us, Susan?" cried several little girls to a schoolmate. "We are going to the woods; do come, too."

2. "I should like to go with you very much," replied Susan, with a sigh; "but I can not finish the task grandmother set me to do."

3. "How tiresome it must be to stay at home to work on a holiday!" said one of the girls, with a toss of her head. "Susan's grandmother is too strict."

4. Susan heard this remark, and, as she bent her head over her task, she wiped away a tear, and thought of the pleasant afternoon the girls would spend gathering wild flowers in the woods.

5. Soon she said to herself, "What harm can there be in moving the mark grandmother put in the stocking? The woods must be very beautiful to-day, and how I should like to be in them!"

6. "Grandmother," said she, a few minutes afterwards, "I am ready, now." "What, so soon, Susan?" Her grandmother took the work, and looked at it very closely.

"No Crown for Me," Lesson 69, in *McGuffey's Third Eclectic Reader,* ed. William Holmes McGuffey (New York: American Book Company, 1879), 180–84.

7. "True, Susan," said she, laying great stress on each word; "true, I count twenty turns from the mark; and, as you have never deceived me, you may go and amuse yourself as you like the rest of the day."

8. Susan's cheeks were scarlet, and she did not say, "Thank you." As she left the cottage, she walked slowly away, not singing as usual.

9. "Why, here is Susan!" the girls cried, when she joined their company; "but what is the matter? Why have you left your dear, old grandmother?" they tauntingly added.

10. "There is nothing the matter." As Susan repeated these words, she felt that she was trying to deceive herself. She had acted a lie. At the same time she remembered her grandmother's words, "You have never deceived me."

11. "Yes, I have deceived her," said she to herself. "If she knew all, she would never trust me again."

12. When the little party had reached an open space in the woods, her companions ran about enjoying themselves; but Susan sat on the grass, wishing she were at home confessing her fault.

13. After a while Rose cried out, "Let us make a crown of violets, and put it on the head of the best girl here."

14. "It will be easy enough to make the crown, but not so easy to decide who is to wear it," said Julia.

15. "Why, Susan is to wear it, of course," said Rose: "is she not said to be the best girl in school, and the most obedient at home?"

16. "Yes, yes; the crown shall be for Susan," cried the other girls, and they began to make the crown. It was soon finished.

17. "Now, Susan," said Rose, "put it on in a very dignified way, for you are to be our queen."

18. As these words were spoken, the crown was placed on her head. In a moment she snatched it off, and threw it on the ground, saying, "No crown for me; I do not deserve it."

19. The girls looked at her with surprise. "I have deceived my grandmother," said she, while tears flowed down her cheeks. "I altered the mark she put in the stocking, that I might join you in the woods."

20. "Do you call that wicked?" asked one of the girls.

"I am quite sure it is; and I have been miserable all the time I have been here."

21. Susan now ran home, and as soon as she got there she said, with a beating heart, "O grandmother! I deserve to be punished, for I altered the mark you put in the stocking. Do forgive me; I am very sorry and unhappy."

22. "Susan," said her grandmother, "I knew it all the time; but I let you go out, hoping that your own conscience would tell you of your sin. I am so glad that you have confessed your fault and your sorrow."

23. "When shall I be your own little girl again?" "Now," was the quick reply, and Susan's grandmother kissed her forehead.

The Good Son

1. There was once a jeweler, noted for many virtues. One day, the Jewish elders came to him to buy some diamonds, to put upon that part of the dress of their high-priest, which the Bible calls an ephod.

2. They told him what they wanted, and offered him a fair price for the diamonds. He replied that he could not let them see the jewels at that moment, and requested them to call again.

"The Good Son," Lesson 10, in *McGuffey's Fourth Eclectic Reader,* ed. William Holmes McGuffey (New York: American Book Company, 1879), 44–45.

3. As they wanted them without delay, and thought that the object of the jeweler was only to increase the price of the diamonds, the elders offered him twice, then three times, as much as they were worth. But he still refused, and they went away in very bad humor.

4. Some hours after, he went to them, and placed before them the diamonds, for which they again offered him the last price they had named; but he said, "I will only accept the first one you offered to me this morning."

5. "Why, then, did you not close with us at once?" asked they in surprise. "When you came," replied he, "my father had the key of the chest, in which the diamonds were kept, and as he was asleep, I should have been obliged to wake him to obtain them.

6. "At his age, a short hour of sleep does him a great deal of good; and for all the gold in the world, I would not be wanting in respect to my father, or take from him a single comfort."

7. The elders, affected by these feeling words, spread their hands upon the jeweler's head, and said, "Thou shalt be blessed of Him who has said, 'Honor thy father and thy mother;' and thy children shall one day pay thee the same respect and love thou hast shown to thy father."

6
Education

In a famous nineteenth-century lithograph, a railroad streaks across the plains toward majestic mountains, while in the foreground hardy pioneers build a new Western town. In the middle of this beehive of activity stands a cabin with a sign that reads "public school." Education was not just about learning to read and write. It was a poetic ideal, a font of social mobility, a source of technological progress, and a foundation for democratic institutions. The lesson "I Will Think of It" presents the world of thought as a human resource; men like Galileo, Isaac Newton, and James Watt improved life simply by exercising their intelligence, and school children were urged to emulate them. Education was central to the entire worldview of the McGuffey readers. In "The Truant," doing well in school is linked to honoring one's parents; "Advantages of Industry" declares that studying hard is doing God's will; "Emulation" emphasizes the importance of taking care of others; and "Necessity of Education" insists that without literary and religious institutions, even great nations lose their way. (The original title of this last essay was "A Plea for the West," and it was widely reprinted in the nineteenth century. See pp. 99–101.) Do you think that nineteenth-century students found education to be as fulfilling as the McGuffeys promised?

The Truant

1. James Brown was ten years old when his parents sent him to school. It was not far from his home, and therefore they sent him by himself.

2. But, instead of going to school, he was in the habit of playing truant. He would go into the fields, or spend his time with idle boys.

"The Truant," Lesson 7, in *McGuffey's Third Eclectic Reader,* ed. William Holmes McGuffey (New York: American Book Company, 1879), 27–29.

3. But this was not all. When he went home, he would falsely tell his mother that he had been to school, and had said his lessons very well.

4. One fine morning, his mother told James to make haste home from school, for she wished, after he had come back, to take him to his aunt's.

5. But, instead of minding her, he went off to the water, where there were some boats. There he met plenty of idle boys.

6. Some of these boys found that James had money, which his aunt had given him; and he was led by them to hire a boat, and to go with them upon the water.

7. Little did James think of the danger into which he was running. Soon the wind began to blow, and none of them knew how to manage the boat.

8. For some time, they struggled against the wind and the tide. At last, they became so tired that they could row no longer.

9. A large wave upset the boat, and they were all thrown into the water. Think of James Brown, the truant, at this time!

10. He was far from home, known by no one. His parents were ignorant of his danger. He was struggling in the water, on the point of being drowned.

11. Some men, however, saw the boys, and went out to them in a boat. They reached them just in time to save them from a watery grave.

12. They were taken into a house, where their clothes were dried. After a while, they were sent home to their parents.

13. James was very sorry for his conduct, and he was never known to be guilty of the same thing again.

14. He became regular at school, learned to attend to his books, and, above all, to obey his parents perfectly.

I Will Think of It

1. "I will think of it." It is easy to say this; but do you know what great things have come from thinking?

2. We can not see our thoughts, or hear, or taste, or feel them; and yet what mighty power they have!

3. Sir Isaac Newton was seated in his garden on a summer's evening, when he saw an apple fall from a tree. He began to *think,* and, in trying

"I Will Think of It," Lesson 39, in *McGuffey's Third Eclectic Reader,* ed. William Holmes McGuffey (New York: American Book Company, 1879), 101–03.

to find out why the apple fell, discovered how the earth, sun, moon, and stars are kept in their places.

4. A boy named James Watt sat quietly by the fireside, watching the lid of the tea-kettle as it moved up and down. He began to *think;* he wanted to find out why the steam in the kettle moved the heavy lid.

5. From that time he went on thinking, and thinking; and when he became a man, he improved the steam-engine so much that it could, with the greatest ease, do the work of many horses.

6. When you see a steam-boat, a steam-mill, or a locomotive, remember that it would never have been built if it had not been for the hard thinking of some one.

7. A man named Galileo was once standing in the cathedral of Pisa, when he saw a chandelier swaying to and fro.

8. This set him *thinking,* and it led to the invention of the pendulum.

9. James Ferguson was a poor Scotch shepherd-boy. Once, seeing the inside of a watch, he was filled with wonder. "Why should I not make a watch?" thought he.

10. But how was he to get the materials out of which to make the wheels and the mainspring? He soon found how to get them: he made the mainspring out of a piece of whalebone. He then made a wooden clock which kept good time.

11. He began, also, to copy pictures with a pen, and portraits with oil-colors. In a few years, while still a small boy, he earned money enough to support his father.

12. When he became a man, he went to London to live. Some of the wisest men in England, and the king himself, used to attend his lectures. His motto was, "I will think of it;" and he made his thoughts useful to himself and the world.

13. Boys, when you have a difficult lesson to learn, don't feel discouraged, and ask some one to help you before helping yourselves. Think, and by thinking you will learn how to think to some purpose.

Consequences of Idleness

1. Many young persons seem to think it of not much consequence if they do not improve their time well in youth, vainly expecting that they can make it up by diligence when they are older. They also think it is disgraceful for men and women to be idle, but that there can be no harm for persons who are young to spend their time in any manner they please.

2. George Jones thought so. When he was twelve years old, he went to an academy to prepare to enter college. His father was at great expense in obtaining books for him, clothing him, and paying his tuition. But George was idle. The preceptor of the academy would often tell him that if he did not study diligently when young he would never succeed well.

3. But George thought of nothing but present pleasure. He would often go to school without having made any preparation for his morning lesson; and, when called to recite with his class, he would stammer and make such blunders that the rest of the class could not help laughing at him. He was one of the poorest scholars in the school, because he was one of the most idle.

4. When recess came, and all the boys ran out of the academy upon the play-ground, idle George would come moping along. Instead of studying diligently while in school, he was indolent and half asleep. When the proper time for play came, he had no relish for it. I recollect very well, that, when "tossing up" for a game of ball, we used to choose every body on the play-ground before we chose George; and if there were enough without him we used to leave him out. Thus he was unhappy in school and out of school.

5. There is nothing which makes a person enjoy play so well as to study hard. When recess was over, and the rest of the boys returned, fresh and vigorous, to their studies, George might be seen lagging and moping along to his seat. Sometimes he would be asleep in school; sometimes he would pass his time in catching flies, and penning them up in little holes, which he cut in his seat; and sometimes, when the preceptor's back was turned, he would throw a paper ball across the room.

6. When the class was called up to recite, George would come drowsily along, looking as mean and ashamed as though he were going to be whipped. The rest of the class stepped up to the recitation with alacrity, and appeared happy and contented. When it came George's turn

"Consequences of Idleness," Lesson 39, in *McGuffey's Fourth Eclectic Reader,* ed. William Holmes McGuffey (New York: American Book Company, 1879), 110–12.

to recite, he would be so long in doing it, and make such blunders, that all most heartily wished him out of the class.

7. At last, George went with his class to enter college. Though he passed a very poor examination, he was admitted with the rest; for those who examined him thought it was possible that the reason why he did not answer questions better was because he was frightened. Now came hard times for poor George. In college there is not much mercy shown to bad scholars; and George had neglected his studies so long that he could not now keep up with his class, let him try ever so hard.

8. He could, without much difficulty, get along in the academy, where there were only two or three boys of his own class to laugh at him. But now he had to go into a large recitation room, filled with students from all parts of the country. In the presence of all these, he must rise and recite to a professor. Poor fellow! He paid dearly for his idleness.

9. You would have pitied him if you could have seen him trembling in his seat, every moment expecting to be called upon to recite. And when he was called upon, he would stand up and take what the class called a "dead set;" that is, he could not recite at all. Sometimes he would make such ludicrous blunders that the whole class would burst into a laugh. Such are the applauses an idler gets. He was wretched, of course. He had been idle so long that he hardly knew how to apply his mind to study. All the good scholars avoided him; they were ashamed to be seen in his company. He became discouraged, and gradually grew dissipated.

10. The officers of the college were soon compelled to suspend him. He returned in a few months, but did no better; and his father was then advised to take him from college. He left college, despised by every one. A few months ago, I met him, a poor wanderer, without money and without friends. Such are the wages of idleness. I hope every reader will, from this history, take warning, and "stamp improvement on the wings of time."

Advantages of Industry

1. I gave you, in the last lesson, the history of George Jones, an idle boy, and showed you the consequences of his idleness. I shall now give you the history of Charles Bullard, a classmate of George. Charles was about the same age as George, and did not possess superior talents.

"Advantages of Industry," Lesson 40, in *McGuffey's Fourth Eclectic Reader,* ed. William Holmes McGuffey (New York: American Book Company, 1879), 113–15.

Indeed, I doubt whether he was equal to him in natural powers of mind.

2. But Charles was a hard student. When quite young, he was always careful and diligent in school. Sometimes, when there was a very hard lesson, instead of going out to play during recess, he would stay in to study. He had resolved that his first object should be to get his lessons well, and then he could play with a good conscience. He loved play as well as any body, and was one of the best players on the ground. I hardly ever saw any boy catch a ball better than he could. When playing any game, every one was glad to get Charles on his side.

3. I have said that Charles would sometimes stay in at recess. This, however, was very seldom; it was only when the lessons were very hard indeed. Generally, he was among the first on the play-ground, and he was also among the first to go into school when called. Hard study gave him a relish for play, and play again gave him a relish for hard study; so he was happy both in school and out. The preceptor could not help liking him, for he always had his lessons well committed, and never gave him any trouble.

4. When he went to enter college, the preceptor gave him a good recommendation. He was able to answer all the questions which were put to him when he was examined. He had studied so well when he was in the academy, and was so thoroughly prepared for college, that he found it very easy to keep up with his class, and had much time for reading interesting books.

5. But he would always get his lesson well before he did any thing else, and would review it just before recitation. When called upon to recite, he rose tranquil and happy, and very seldom made mistakes. The officers of the college had a high opinion of him, and he was respected by all the students.

6. There was, in the college, a society made up of all the best scholars. Charles was chosen a member of that society. It was the custom to choose some one of the society to deliver a public address every year. This honor was conferred on Charles; and he had studied so diligently, and read so much, that he delivered an address which was very interesting to all who heard it.

7. At last he graduated, as it is called; that is, he finished his collegiate course, and received his degree. It was known by all that he was a good scholar, and by all that he was respected. His father and mother, brothers and sisters, came on the commencement day to hear him speak.

8. They all felt gratified, and loved Charles more than ever. Many situations of usefulness and profit were opened to him; for Charles was now an intelligent man, and universally respected. He is still a useful and a happy man. He has a cheerful home, and is esteemed by all who know him.

9. Such are the rewards of industry. How strange it is that any person should be willing to live in idleness, when it will certainly make him unhappy! The idle boy is almost invariably poor and miserable; the industrious boy is happy and prosperous.

10. But perhaps some child who reads this, asks, "Does God notice little children in school?" He certainly does. And if you are not diligent in the improvement of your time, it is one of the surest evidences that your heart is not right with God. You are placed in this world to improve your time. In youth you must be preparing for future usefulness. And if you do not improve the advantages you enjoy, you sin against your Maker.

With books, or work, or healthful play,
Let your first years be past;
That you may give, for every day,
Some good account, at last.

Emulation

1. Frank's father was speaking to a friend, one day, on the subject of competition at school. He said that he could answer for it that envy is not always connected with it.

2. He had been excelled by many, but did not recollect ever having felt envious of his successful rivals; "nor did my winning many a prize from my friend Birch," said he, "ever lessen his friendship for me."

3. In support of the truth of this, a friend who was present related an anecdote which had fallen under his own notice in a school in his neighborhood.

4. At this school the sons of several wealthy farmers, and others, who were poorer, received instruction. Frank listened with great attention while the gentleman gave the following account of the two rivals.

5. It happened that the son of a rich farmer and the son of a poor widow came in competition for the head of their class. They were so nearly equal that the teacher could scarcely decide between them; some days one, and some days the other, gained the head of the class. It was determined by seeing who should be at the head of the class for the greater number of days in the week.

"Emulation," Lesson 48, in *McGuffey's Fourth Eclectic Reader,* ed. William Holmes McGuffey (New York: American Book Company, 1879), 132–34.

6. The widow's son, by the last day's trial, gained the victory, and kept his place the following week, till the school was dismissed for the holidays.

7. When they met again the widow's son did not appear, and the farmer's son, being next to him, might now have been at the head of his class. Instead of seizing the vacant place, however, he went to the widow's house to inquire what could be the cause of her son's absence.

8. Poverty was the cause; the poor woman found that she was not able, with her utmost efforts, to continue to pay for the tuition and books of her son, and so he, poor fellow! had been compelled to give up his schooling, and to return to labor for her support.

9. The farmer's son, out of the allowance of pocket-money which his father gave him, bought all the necessary books and paid for the tuition of his rival. He also permitted him to be brought back again to the head of his class, where he continued for some time, at the expense of his generous rival.

LYMAN BEECHER

Necessity of Education

We must educate! We must educate! or we must perish by our own prosperity. If we do not, short will be our race from the cradle to the grave. If, in our haste to be rich and mighty, we outrun our literary and religious institutions, they will never overtake us; or only come up after the battle of liberty is fought and lost, as spoils to grace the victory, and as resources of inexorable despotism for the perpetuity of our bondage.

But what will become of the West if her prosperity rushes up to such a majesty of power, while those great institutions linger which are necessary to form the mind, and the conscience, and the heart of the vast world? It must not be permitted. And yet what is done must be done quickly; for population will not wait, and commerce will not cast anchor, and manufactures will not shut off the steam, nor shut down the gate, and agriculture, pushed by millions of freemen on their fertile soil, will not withhold her corrupting abundance.

Lyman Beecher, "Necessity of Education," Lesson 59, in *McGuffey's Sixth Eclectic Reader,* ed. William Holmes McGuffey (New York: American Book Company, 1879), 228–31.

And let no man at the East quiet himself, and dream of liberty, whatever may become of the West. Our alliance of blood, and political institutions, and common interests, is such, that we can not stand aloof in the hour of her calamity, should it ever come. Her destiny is our destiny; and the day that her gallant ship goes down, our little boat sinks in the vortex!

The great experiment is now making, and from its extent and rapid filling up, is making in the West, whether the perpetuity of our republican institutions can be reconciled with universal suffrage. Without the education of the head and heart of the nation, they can not be; and the question to be decided is, can the nation, or the vast balance power of it, be so imbued with intelligence and virtue as to bring out, in laws and their administration, a perpetual self-preserving energy. We know that the work is a vast one, and of great difficulty; and yet we believe it can be done.

I am aware that our ablest patriots are looking out on the deep, vexed with storms, with great forebodings and failings of heart, for fear of the things that are coming upon us; and I perceive a spirit of impatience rising, and distrust in respect to the perpetuity of our republic; and I am sure that these fears are well founded, and am glad that they exist. It is the star of hope in our dark horizon. Fear is what we need, as the ship needs wind on a rocking sea, after a storm, to prevent foundering. But when our fear and our efforts shall correspond with our danger, the danger is past.

For it is not the impossibility of self-preservation which threatens us; nor is it the unwillingness of the nation to pay the price of the preservation, as she has paid the price of the purchase of our liberties. It is inattention and inconsideration, protracted till the crisis is past, and the things which belong to our peace are hid from our eyes. And blessed be God, that the tokens of a national waking up, the harbinger of God's mercy, are multiplying upon us!

We did not, in the darkest hour, believe that God had brought our fathers to this goodly land to lay the foundation of religious liberty, and wrought such wonders in their preservation, and raised their descendants to such heights of civil and religious liberty, only to reverse the analogy of his providence, and abandon his work.

And though there now be clouds, and the sea roaring, and men's hearts failing, we believe there is light behind the cloud, and that the imminence of our danger is intended, under the guidance of Heaven, to call forth and apply a holy, fraternal fellowship between the East and the West, which shall secure our preservation, and make the prosperity of our nation durable as time, and as abundant as the waves of the sea.

I would add, as a motive to immediate action, that if we do fail in our great experiment of self-government, our destruction will be as signal as the birthright abandoned, the mercies abused, and the provocation offered to beneficent Heaven. The descent of desolation will correspond with the past elevation.

No punishments of Heaven are so severe as those for mercies abused; and no instrumentality employed in their infliction is so dreadful as the wrath of man. No spasms are like the spasms of expiring liberty, and no wailing such as her convulsions extort.

It took Rome three hundred years to die; and our death, if we perish, will be as much more terrific as our intelligence and free institutions have given us more bone, sinew, and vitality. May God hide from me the day when the dying agonies of my country shall begin! O thou beloved land, bound together by the ties of brotherhood, and common interest, and perils! live forever—one and undivided!

7
Men and Women

The McGuffeys were filled with ideas about proper behavior for men and women. Girls were urged to work as hard and do as well in school as boys, but girls and boys were not the same. "Susie Sunbeam" got her name because of her knack for bringing joy into people's lives; we can imagine her growing into a nurturing Victorian woman. A Sammy Sunbeam, on the other hand, might have been thought not quite fully masculine. The bourgeois version of manliness that the McGuffey readers helped spread centered around self-possession, self-control, and following the voice of one's conscience. Manly boys shunned displays of violence or bravado; true courage demonstrated responsibility; bravery meant not just physical but moral fortitude. The height of womanly virtue, however, was expressed in a mother's love for her children, in the private realm of the family. Wives and mothers not only were expected to do the household work for the men who went out into the world of business and public affairs, they also were expected to soothe men's pain. Certainly not all women accepted this situation, but the McGuffeys contain no hint of protest against "separate spheres" for the sexes or the "cult of true womanhood," as the domestic ideal has been called. Do you think that Victorian men and women were comfortable with the roles assigned them by society?

Susie Sunbeam

1. Susie Sunbeam was not her real name; that was Susan Brown. But every one called her Susie Sunbeam, because she had such a sweet, smiling face, and always brought brightness with her when she came.

"Susie Sunbeam," Lesson 12, in *McGuffey's Second Eclectic Reader,* ed. William Holmes McGuffey (New York: American Book Company, 1879), 30–33.

2. Her grandfather first gave her this name, and it seemed to fit the little girl so nicely that soon it took the place of her own.

3. Even when a baby, Susie laughed and crowed from morning till night. No one ever heard her cry unless she was sick or hurt.

4. When she had learned to walk, she loved to go about the house and get things for her mother, and in this way save her as many steps as she could.

5. She would sit by her mother's side for an hour at a time, and ask her ever so many questions, or she would take her new book and read.

6. Susie was always pleasant in her play with other children. She never used an unkind word, but tried to do whatever would please her playmates best.

7. One day, a poor little girl with a very ragged dress was going by, and Susie heard some children teasing her and making fun of her.

8. She at once ran out to the gate, and asked the poor little girl to come in. "What are you crying for?" Susie asked.

9. "Because they all laugh at me," she said.

10. Then Susie took the little girl into the house. She cheered her up with kind words, and gave her a nice dress and a pair of shoes.

11. This brought real joy and gladness to the poor child, and she, too, thought that Susie was rightly called Sunbeam.

Courage and Cowardice

1. Robert and Henry were going home from school, when, on turning a corner, Robert cried out, "A fight! let us go and see!"

2. "No," said Henry; "let us go quietly home and not meddle with this quarrel. We have nothing to do with it, and may get into mischief."

3. "You are a coward, and afraid to go," said Robert, and off he ran. Henry went straight home, and in the afternoon went to school, as usual.

4. But Robert had told all the boys that Henry was a coward, and they laughed at him a great deal.

5. Henry had learned, however, that true courage is shown most in bearing reproach when not deserved, and that he ought to be afraid of nothing but doing wrong.

"Courage and Cowardice," Lesson 30, in *McGuffey's Third Eclectic Reader,* ed. William Holmes McGuffey (New York: American Book Company, 1879), 76–78.

6. A few days after, Robert was bathing with some school-mates, and got out of his depth. He struggled, and screamed for help, but all in vain.

7. The boys who had called Henry a coward, got out of the water as fast as they could, but they did not even try to help him.

8. Robert was fast sinking, when Henry threw off his clothes, and sprang into the water. He reached Robert just as he was sinking the last time.

9. By great effort, and with much danger to himself, he brought Robert to the shore, and thus saved his life.

10. Robert and his school-mates were ashamed at having called Henry a coward. They owned that he had more courage than any of them.

11. Never be afraid to do good, but always fear to do evil.

MRS. M. O. JOHNSON

True Manliness

1. "Please, mother, do sit down and let me try my hand," said Fred Liscom, a bright, active boy twelve years old. Mrs. Liscom, looking pale and worn, was moving languidly about, trying to clear away the breakfast she had scarcely tasted.

2. She smiled, and said, "You, Fred, you wash dishes?" "Yes, indeed, mother," replied Fred; "I should be a poor scholar if I couldn't, when I've seen you do it so many times. Just try me."

3. A look of relief came over his mother's face as she seated herself in her low rocking-chair. Fred washed the dishes, and put them in the closet. He then swept the kitchen, brought up the potatoes from the cellar for the dinner and washed them, and then set out for school.

4. Fred's father was away from home, and as there was some cold meat in the pantry, Mrs. Liscom found it an easy task to prepare dinner. Fred hurried home from school, set the table, and again washed the dishes.

5. He kept on in this way for two or three days, when his mother was able to resume her usual work, and he felt amply rewarded when the doctor, who happened in one day, said, "Well, madam, it's my opinion that you would have been very sick if you had not kept quiet."

Mrs. M. O. Johnson, "True Manliness," Lesson 14, in *McGuffey's Fourth Eclectic Reader*, ed. William Holmes McGuffey (New York: American Book Company, 1879), 50–52.

6. The doctor did not know how the "quiet" had been secured, nor how the boy's heart bounded at his words. Fred had given up a great deal of what boys hold dear, for the purpose of helping his mother, coasting and skating being just at this time in perfection.

7. Besides this, his temper and his patience had been severely tried. He had been in the habit of going early to school, and staying to play after it was dismissed.

8. The boys missed him, and their curiosity was excited when he would give no other reason for not coming to school earlier, or staying after school, than that he was "wanted at home." "I'll tell you," said Tom Barton, "I'll find him out, boys—see if I don't!"

9. So he called for Fred to go to school, and on his way to the side door walked lightly and somewhat nearer the kitchen window than was absolutely needful. Looking in, he saw Fred standing at the table with a dish-cloth in his hand.

10. Of course he reported this at school, and various were the greetings poor Fred received at recess. "Well, you're a brave one to stay at home washing dishes." "Girl-boy!" "Pretty Bessie!" "Lost your apron, haven't you, Polly!"

11. Fred was not wanting either in spirit or courage, and he was strongly tempted to resent these insults and to fight some of his tormentors. But his consciousness of right and his love for his mother helped him.

12. While he was struggling for self-mastery, his teacher appeared at the door of the school-house. Fred caught his eye, and it seemed to look, if it did not say, "Don't give up! Be really brave!" He knew the teacher had heard the insulting taunts of his thoughtless school-mates.

13. The boys received notice during the day that Fred must not be taunted or teased in any manner. They knew that the teacher meant what he said; and so the brave little boy had no farther trouble.

True Manliness

(Concluded)

1. "Fire! fire!" The cry crept out on the still night air, and the fire bells began to ring. Fred was wakened by the alarm and the red light streaming into his room. He dressed himself in a moment, almost, and tapped at the door of his mother's bedroom.

2. "It is Mr. Barton's house, mother. Do let me go," he said in eager, excited tones. Mrs. Liscom thought a moment. He was young, but she could trust him, and she knew how much his heart was in the request.

3. "Yes, you may go," she answered; "but be careful, my boy. If you

Mrs. M. O. Johnson, "True Manliness (Concluded)," Lesson 15, in *McGuffey's Fourth Eclectic Reader,* ed. William Holmes McGuffey (New York: American Book Company, 1879), 52–54.

can help, do so; but do nothing rashly." Fred promised to follow her advice, and hurried to the fire.

4. Mr. and Mrs. Barton were not at home. The house had been left in charge of the servants. The fire spread with fearful speed, for there was a high wind, and it was found impossible to save the house. The servants ran about, screaming and lamenting, but doing nothing to any purpose.

5. Fred found Tom outside, in safety. "Where is Katy?" he asked. Tom, trembling with terror, seemed to have had no thought but of his own escape. He said, "Katy is in the house!" "In what room?" asked Fred. "In that one," pointing to a window in the upper story.

6. It was no time for words, but for instant, vigorous action. The staircase was already on fire; there was but one way to reach Katy, and that full of danger. The second floor might fall at any moment, and Fred knew it. But he trusted in an arm stronger than his own, and silently sought help and guidance.

7. A ladder was quickly brought, and placed against the house. Fred mounted it, followed by the hired man, dashed in the sash of the window, and pushed his way into the room where the poor child lay nearly suffocated with smoke.

8. He roused her with some difficulty, carried her to the window, and placed her upon the sill. She was instantly grasped by strong arms, and carried down the ladder, Fred following as fast as possible. They had scarcely reached the ground before a crash of falling timbers told them that they had barely escaped with their lives.

9. Tom Barton never forgot the lesson of that night; and he came to believe, and to act upon the belief, in after years, that true manliness is in harmony with gentleness, kindness, and self-denial.

ELIZABETH AKERS ALLEN

Rock Me to Sleep

1. Backward, turn backward, O Time, in your flight,
   Make me a child again, just for to-night!
   Mother, come back from the echoless shore,
   Take me again to your heart as of yore;
   Kiss from my forehead the furrows of care,
   Smooth the few silver threads out of my hair;
   Over my slumbers your loving watch keep;—
   Rock me to sleep, mother,—rock me to sleep!

2. Backward, flow backward, O tide of the years!
   I am so weary of toil and of tears;
   Toil without recompense, tears all in vain;
   Take them, and give me my childhood again!
   I have grown weary of dust and decay,—
   Weary of flinging my soul-wealth away;
   Weary of sowing for others to reap;—
   Rock me to sleep, mother,—rock me to sleep!

3. Tired of the hollow, the base, the untrue,
   Mother, O mother, my heart calls for you!
   Many a summer the grass has grown green,
   Blossomed and faded, our faces between:
   Yet with strong yearning and passionate pain,
   Long I to-night for your presence again.
   Come from the silence so long and so deep;—
   Rock me to sleep, mother,—rock me to sleep!

4. Over my heart in the days that are flown,
   No love like mother-love ever has shone;
   No other worship abides and endures,
   Faithful, unselfish, and patient like yours:
   None like a mother can charm away pain
   From the sick soul, and the world-weary brain.
   Slumber's soft calms o'er my heavy lids creep;—
   Rock me to sleep, mother,—rock me to sleep!

Elizabeth Akers Allen, "Rock Me to Sleep," Lesson 94, in *McGuffey's Fifth Eclectic Reader*, ed. William Holmes McGuffey (New York: American Book Company, 1879), 286–88.

5. Come, let your brown hair, just lighted with gold,
   Fall on your shoulders again, as of old;
   Let it drop over my forehead to-night,
   Shading my faint eyes away from the light;
   For with its sunny-edged shadows once more,
   Haply will throng the sweet visions of yore;
   Lovingly, softly, its bright billows sweep;—
   Rock me to sleep, mother,—rock me to sleep!

6. Mother, dear mother, the years have been long
   Since I last listened your lullaby song;
   Sing, then, and unto my soul it shall seem
   Womanhood's years have been only a dream;
   Clasped to your heart in a loving embrace,
   With your light lashes just sweeping my face,
   Never hereafter to wake or to weep;—
   Rock me to sleep, mother,—rock me to sleep!

GEORGE P. MORRIS

My Mother's Bible

1. This book is all that's left me now,—
      Tears will unbidden start,—
   With faltering lip and throbbing brow
      I press it to my heart.
   For many generations past
      Here is our family tree;
   My mother's hands this Bible clasped,
      She, dying, gave it me.

2. Ah! well do I remember those
      Whose names these records bear;
   Who round the hearth-stone used to close,
      After the evening prayer,

George P. Morris, "My Mother's Bible," Lesson 117, in *McGuffey's Fifth Eclectic Reader,* ed. William Holmes McGuffey (New York: American Book Company, 1879), 351–52.

And speak of what these pages said
In tones my heart would thrill!
Though they are with the silent dead,
Here are they living still!

3. My father read this holy book
To brothers, sisters, dear;
How calm was my poor mother's look,
Who loved God's word to hear!
Her angel face,—I see it yet!
What thronging memories come!
Again that little group is met
Within the walls of home!

4. Thou truest friend man ever knew,
Thy constancy I've tried;
When all were false, I found thee true,
My counselor and guide.
The mines of earth no treasures give
That could this volume buy;
In teaching me the way to live,
It taught me how to die.

FRANCIS HOPKINSON

House-Cleaning

There is no season of the year in which the lady may not, if she pleases, claim her privilege; but the latter end of May is generally fixed upon for the purpose. The attentive husband may judge, by certain prognostics, when the storm is at hand. If the lady grows uncommonly fretful, finds fault with the servants, is discontented with the children, and complains much of the nastiness of every thing about her, these are symptoms which ought not to be neglected, yet they sometimes go off without any further effect.

But if, when the husband rises in the morning, he should observe in the

Francis Hopkinson, "House-Cleaning," Lesson 6, in *McGuffey's Sixth Eclectic Reader,* ed. William Holmes McGuffey (New York: American Book Company, 1879), 73–77.

yard a wheel-barrow with a quantity of lime in it, or should see certain buckets filled with a solution of lime in water, there is no time for hesitation. He immediately locks up the apartment or closet where his papers and private property are kept, and, putting the key in his pocket, betakes himself to flight. A husband, however beloved, becomes a perfect nuisance during this season of female rage. His authority is superseded, his commission suspended, and the very scullion who cleans the brasses in the kitchen becomes of more importance than he. He has nothing for it but to abdicate for a time, and run from an evil which he can neither prevent nor mollify.

The husband gone, the ceremony begins. The walls are stripped of their furniture—paintings, prints, and looking-glasses lie huddled in heaps about the floors; the curtains are torn from their testers, the beds crammed into windows, chairs and tables, bedsteads and cradles, crowd the yard, and the garden fence bends beneath the weight of carpets, blankets, cloth cloaks, old coats, under petticoats, and ragged breeches. Here may be seen the lumber of the kitchen, forming a dark and confused mass for the foreground of the picture; gridirons and frying-pans, rusty shovels and broken tongs, joint stools, and the fractured remains of rush-bottomed chairs. There a closet has disgorged its bowels—riveted plates and dishes, halves of china bowls, cracked tumblers, broken wine-glasses, phials of forgotten physic, papers of unknown powders, seeds and dried herbs, tops of tea-pots, and stoppers of departed decanters—from the rag-hole in the garret, to the rat-hole in the cellar, no place escapes unrummaged. It would seem as if the day of general doom had come, and the utensils of the house were dragged forth to judgment.

In this tempest, the words of King Lear unavoidably present themselves, and might, with little alteration, be made strictly applicable.

"Let the great gods,
That keep this dreadful pother o'er our heads,
Find out their enemies now. Tremble, thou wretch,
That hast within thee undivulged crimes
Unwhipp'd of justice.
Close pent-up guilts,
Rive your concealing continents, and cry
These dreadful summoners grace."

This ceremony completed, and the house thoroughly evacuated, the next operation is to smear the walls and ceilings with brushes dipped into a solution of lime, called whitewash; to pour buckets of water over every floor; and scratch all the partitions and wainscots with hard brushes, charged with soft-soap and stone-cutters' sand.

The windows by no means escape the general deluge. A servant scrambles out upon the pent-house, at the risk of her neck, and, with a mug in her hand and a bucket within reach, dashes innumerable gallons of water against the glass panes, to the great annoyance of passengers in the street.

I have been told that an action at law was once brought against one of these water nymphs, by a person who had a new suit of clothes spoiled by this operation: but after long argument, it was determined that no damages could be awarded; inasmuch as the defendant was in the exercise of a legal right, and not answerable for the consequences. And so the poor gentleman was doubly nonsuited; for he lost both his suit of clothes and his suit at law.

These smearings and scratchings, these washings and dashings, being duly performed, the next ceremonial is to cleanse and replace the distracted furniture. You may have seen a house-raising, or a ship launch—recollect, if you can, the hurry, bustle, confusion, and noise of such a scene, and you will have some idea of this cleansing match. The misfortune is, that the sole object is to make things *clean.* It matters not how many useful, ornamental, or valuable articles suffer mutilation or death under the operation. A mahogany chair and a carved frame undergo the same discipline; they are to be made *clean* at all events; but their preservation is not worthy of attention.

For instance: a fine large engraving is laid flat upon the floor; a number of smaller prints are piled upon it, until the superincumbent weight cracks the lower glass—but this is of no importance. A valuable picture is placed leaning against the sharp corner of a table; others are made to lean against that, till the pressure of the whole forces the corner of the table through the canvas of the first. The frame and glass of a fine print are to be cleaned; the spirit and oil used on this occasion are suffered to leak through and deface the engraving—no matter. If the glass is clean and the frame shines, it is sufficient—the rest is not worthy of consideration. An able arithmetician hath made a calculation, founded on long experience, and proved that the losses and destruction incident to two whitewashings are equal to one removal, and three removals equal to one fire.

This cleansing frolic over, matters begin to resume their pristine appearance: the storm abates, and all would be well again: but it is impossible that so great a convulsion in so small a community should pass over without producing some consequences. For two or three weeks after the operation, the family are usually afflicted with sore eyes, sore throats, or severe colds, occasioned by exhalations from wet floors and damp walls.

I know a gentleman, here, who is fond of accounting for every thing in a philosophical way. He considers this, what I call a *custom,* as a real periodical *disease* peculiar to the climate. His train of reasoning is whimsical and ingenious, but I am not at leisure to give you the detail. The result was, that he found the distemper to be incurable; but after much study, he thought he had discovered a method to divert the evil he could not subdue. For this purpose, he caused a small building, about twelve feet square, to be erected in his garden, and furnished with some ordinary chairs and tables, and a few prints of the cheapest sort. His hope was, that when the whitewashing frenzy seized the females of his family, they might repair to this apartment, and scrub, and scour, and smear to their hearts' content; and so spend the violence of the disease in this outpost, whilst he enjoyed himself in quiet at headquarters. But the experiment did not answer his expectation. It was impossible it should, since a principal part of the gratification consists in the lady's having an uncontrolled right to torment her husband at least once in every year; to turn him out of doors, and take the reins of government into her own hands.

There is a much better contrivance than this of the philosopher's; which is, to cover the walls of the house with paper. This is generally done. And though it does not abolish, it at least shortens the period of female dominion. This paper is decorated with various fancies; and made so ornamental that the women have admitted the fashion without perceiving the design.

There is also another alleviation to the husband's distress. He generally has the sole use of a small room or closet for his books and papers, the key of which he is allowed to keep. This is considered as a privileged place, even in the whitewashing season, and stands like the land of Goshen[1] amidst the plagues of Egypt.[2] But then he must be extremely cautious, and ever upon his guard; for, should he inadvertently go abroad and leave the key in his door, the house-maid, who is always on the watch for such an opportunity, immediately enters in triumph, with buckets, brooms, and brushes—takes possession of the premises, and forthwith puts all his books and papers "to rights," to his utter confusion, and sometimes serious detriment.

[1]The corner of the Nile delta out of which Moses led the Israelites.

[2]The pestilence and calamities imposed by God on Egypt during the time of the Jews' bondage.

8
Religion

Americans in the nineteenth century interpreted the constitutional separation of church and state rather narrowly. There must be no established church (like the Church of England, for example), but most people felt that state-supported institutions like schools should be strongly influenced by religion. While America had no national church, the various Protestant denominations (Baptist, Methodist, Episcopal, Presbyterian, Congregational, and so forth) implicitly comprised a consensus. These groups sometimes disagreed among themselves, but they generally rejected the Catholic Church, with its Latin Mass, hierarchy of pope, cardinals, and bishops, and its belief that priests mediate between each individual and God. Protestants insisted that salvation required each individual to confront the Word of God directly, so public education, then, took on special importance. Even religion did not remain isolated from other social ideals. "You will not often find," declares Gardiner Spring in the lesson "Observance of the Sabbath," "a notorious Sabbath-breaker a permanently prosperous man; and a Sabbath-breaking community is never a happy or prosperous community." What connections do you see between Christian values and other social goals in the following selections?

God Is Great and Good

1. I know God made the sun
   To fill the day with light;
He made the twinkling stars
   To shine all through the night.

"God Is Great and Good," Lesson 56, in *McGuffey's Second Eclectic Reader,* ed. William Holmes McGuffey (New York: American Book Company, 1879), 119–20.

2. He made the hills that rise
   So very high and steep;
He made the lakes and seas,
   That are so broad and deep.

3. He made the streams so wide,
   That flow through wood and vale;
He made the rills so small,
   That leap down hill and dale.

4. He made each bird that sings
   So sweetly all the day;
He made each flower that springs
   So bright, so fresh, so gay.

5. And He who made all these,
   He made both you and me;
Oh, let us thank Him, then,
   For great and good is He.

Things to Remember

1. When you rise in the morning, remember who kept you from danger during the night. Remember who watched over you while you slept, and whose sun shines around you, and gives you the sweet light of day.

2. Let God have the thanks of your heart, for his kindness and his care; and pray for his protection during the wakeful hours of day.

3. Remember that God made all creatures to be happy, and will do nothing that may prevent their being so, without good reason for it.

4. When you are at the table, do not eat in a greedy manner, like a pig. Eat quietly, and do not reach forth your hand for the food, but ask some one to help you.

5. Do not become peevish and pout, because you do not get a part of every thing. Be satisfied with what is given you.

6. Avoid a pouting face, angry looks, and angry words. Do not slam

"Things to Remember," Lesson 25, in *McGuffey's Third Eclectic Reader,* ed. William Holmes McGuffey (New York: American Book Company, 1879), 65–67.

the doors. Go quietly up and down stairs; and never make a loud noise about the house.

7. Be kind and gentle in your manners; not like the howling winter storm, but like the bright summer's morning.

8. Do always as your parents bid you. Obey them with a ready mind, and with a pleasant face.

9. Never do any thing that you would be afraid or ashamed that your parents should know. Remember, if no one else sees you, God does, from whom you can not hide even your most secret thought.

10. At night, before you go to sleep, think whether you have done any thing that was wrong during the day, and pray to God to forgive you. If any one has done you wrong, forgive him in your heart.

11. If you have not learned something useful, or been in some way useful, during the past day, think that it is a day lost, and be very sorry for it.

12. Trust in the Lord, and He will guide you in the way of good men. The path of the just is as the shining light that shineth more and more unto the perfect day.

13. We must do all the good we can to all men, for this is well pleasing in the sight of God. He delights to see his children walk in love, and do good one to another.

The Lord's Prayer

1. Our Father in heaven,
   We hallow thy name;
   May thy kingdom holy
   On earth be the same;
   Oh, give to us daily
   Our portion of bread;
   It is from thy bounty,
   That all must be fed.

2. Forgive our transgressions,
   And teach us to know
   The humble compassion
   That pardons each foe;

"The Lord's Prayer," Lesson 35, in *McGuffey's Third Eclectic Reader,* ed. William Holmes McGuffey (New York: American Book Company, 1879), 90.

Keep us from temptation,
From weakness and sin,
And thine be the glory
Forever! Amen!

Who Made the Stars?

1. "Mother, who made the stars, which light
The beautiful blue sky?
Who made the moon, so clear and bright,
That rises up so high?"

2. " 'Twas God, my child, the Glorious One,
He formed them by his power;
He made alike the brilliant sun,
And every leaf and flower.

3. "He made your little feet to walk;
Your sparkling eyes to see;
Your busy, prattling tongue to talk,
And limbs so light and free.

4. "He paints each fragrant flower that blows,
With loveliness and bloom;
He gives the violet and the rose
Their beauty and perfume.

5. "Our various wants his hands supply;
He guides us every hour;
We're kept beneath his watchful eye,
And guarded by his power.

6. "Then let your little heart, my love,
Its grateful homage pay
To that kind Friend, who, from above,
Thus guides you every day.

"Who Made the Stars?" Lesson 48, in *McGuffey's Third Eclectic Reader,* ed. William Holmes McGuffey (New York: American Book Company, 1879), 126–27.

7. "In all the changing scenes of time,
   On Him our hopes depend;
In every age, in every clime,
   Our Father and our Friend."

The Golden Rule

1. To act with integrity and good faith was such a habit with Susan that she had never before thought of examining the Golden Rule: "All things whatsoever ye would that men should do to you, do ye even so to them." But the longer she reflected upon it, the stronger was her conviction that she did not always obey the precept; at length, she appealed to her mother for its meaning.

2. "It implies," said her mother, "in the first place, a total destruction of all selfishness: for a man who loves himself better than his neighbors, can never do to others as he would have others do to him. We are bound not only to do, but to feel, toward others as we would have others feel toward us. Remember, it is much easier to reprove the sin of others than to overcome temptation when it assails ourselves.

3. "A man may be perfectly honest and yet very selfish; but the command implies something more than mere honesty; it requires charity as well as integrity. The meaning of the command is fully explained in the parable of the Good Samaritan. The Levite, who passed by the wounded man without offering him assistance, may have been a man of great honesty; but he did not do unto the poor stranger as he would have wished others to do unto him."

4. Susan pondered carefully and seriously on what her mother had said. When she thought over her past conduct, a blush of shame crept to her cheeks, and a look of sorrow into her eyes, as many little acts of selfishness and unkindness came back to her memory. She resolved that for the future, both in great things and small, she would remember and follow the Golden Rule.

5. It was not long after this that an opportunity occurred of trying Susan's principles. One Saturday evening when she went, as usual, to farmer Thompson's inn, to receive the price of her mother's washing for

"The Golden Rule," Lesson 51, in *McGuffey's Fourth Eclectic Reader,* ed. William Holmes McGuffey (New York: American Book Company, 1879), 139–43.

the boarders, which amounted to five dollars, she found the farmer in the stable-yard.

6. He was apparently in a terrible rage with some horse-dealers with whom he had been bargaining. He held in his hand an open pocket-book, full of bills; and scarcely noticing the child as she made her request, except to swear at her, as usual, for troubling him when he was busy, he handed her a bank-note.

7. Glad to escape so easily, Susan hurried out of the gate, and then, pausing to pin the money safely in the folds of her shawl, she discovered that he had given her two bills instead of one. She looked around; nobody was near to share her discovery; and her first impulse was joy at the unexpected prize.

8. "It is mine, all mine," said she to herself; "I will buy mother a new cloak with it, and she can give her old one to sister Mary, and then Mary can go to the Sunday-school with me next winter. I wonder if it will not buy a pair of shoes for brother Tom, too."

9. At that moment she remembered that he must have given it to her by mistake; and therefore she had no right to it. But again the voice of the tempter whispered, "He gave it, and how do you know that he did not intend to make you a present of it? Keep it; he will never know it, even if it should be a mistake; for he had too many such bills in that great pocket-book to miss one."

10. While this conflict was going on in her mind between good and evil, she was hurrying homeward as fast as possible. Yet, before she came in sight of her home, she had repeatedly balanced the comforts which the money would buy against the sin of wronging her neighbor.

11. As she crossed the little bridge over the narrow creek before her mother's door, her eye fell upon a rustic seat which they had occupied during the conversation I have before narrated. Instantly the words of Scripture, "Whatsoever ye would that men should do to you, do ye even so to them," sounded in her ears like a trumpet.

12. Turning suddenly round, as if flying from some unseen peril, the child hastened along the road with breathless speed until she found herself once more at farmer Thompson's gate. "What do you want now?" asked the gruff old fellow, as he saw her again at his side.

13. "Sir, you paid me two bills, instead of one," said she, trembling in every limb. "Two bills? did I? let me see; well, so I did; but did you just find it out? Why did you not bring it back sooner?" Susan blushed and hung her head.

14. "You wanted to keep it, I suppose," said he. "Well, I am glad your mother was more honest than you, or I should have been five dollars

poorer and none the wiser." "My mother knows nothing about it, sir," said Susan; "I brought it back before I went home."

15. The old man looked at the child, and, as he saw the tears rolling down her cheeks, he seemed touched by her distress. Putting his hand in his pocket, he drew out a shilling and offered it to her.

16. "No, sir, I thank you," sobbed she; "I do not want to be paid for doing right; I only wish you would not think me dishonest, for, indeed, it was a sore temptation. Oh! sir, if you had ever seen those you love best wanting the common comforts of life, you would know how hard it is for us always to do unto others as we would have others do unto us."

17. The heart of the selfish man was touched. "There be things which are little upon the earth, but they are exceeding wise," murmured he, as he bade the little girl good-night, and entered his house a sadder, and, it is to be hoped, a better man. Susan returned to her humble home with a lightened heart, and through the course of a long and useful life she never forgot her first temptation.

The Sermon on the Mount

1. And seeing the multitudes, he went up into a mountain: and when he was set, his disciples came unto him; and he opened his mouth and taught them, saying,

2. Blessed are the poor in spirit; for theirs is the kingdom of heaven. Blessed are they that mourn; for they shall be comforted. Blessed are the meek; for they shall inherit the earth.

3. Blessed are they which do hunger and thirst after righteousness; for they shall be filled. Blessed are the merciful; for they shall obtain mercy. Blessed are the pure in heart; for they shall see God.

4. Blessed are the peace-makers; for they shall be called the children of God. Blessed are they which are persecuted for righteousness' sake; for theirs is the kingdom of heaven.

5. Blessed are ye when men shall revile you, and persecute you, and shall say all manner of evil against you falsely, for my sake. Rejoice and be exceeding glad; for great is your reward in heaven.

"The Sermon on the Mount," Lesson 73, in *McGuffey's Fourth Eclectic Reader,* ed. William Holmes McGuffey (New York: American Book Company, 1879), 204–06.

6. Ye have heard that it hath been said by them of old time, Thou shalt not forswear thyself, but shalt perform unto the Lord thine oaths: but I say unto you, Swear not at all; neither by heaven; for it is God's throne: nor by the earth; for it is his footstool: neither by Jerusalem; for it is the city of the great King.

7. Neither shalt thou swear by thy head, because thou canst not make one hair white or black. But let your communication be, Yea, yea; Nay, nay: for whatsoever is more than these cometh of evil.

8. Ye have heard that it hath been said, An eye for an eye, and a tooth for a tooth: but I say unto you, That ye resist not evil; but whosoever shall smite thee on thy right cheek, turn to him the other also. And if any man will sue thee at the law, and take away thy coat, let him have thy cloak also. And whosoever shall compel thee to go a mile, go with him twain. Give to him that asketh thee, and from him that would borrow of thee turn not thou away.

9. Ye have heard that it hath been said, Thou shalt love thy neighbor and hate thine enemy: but I say unto you, Love your enemies; bless them that curse you, do good to them that hate you, and pray for them which despitefully use you and persecute you; that ye may be the children of your Father which is in heaven: for he maketh his sun to rise on the evil and on the good, and sendeth rain on the just and on the unjust.

10. For if ye love them which love you, what reward have ye? do not even the publicans the same? And if ye salute your brethren only, what do ye more than others? do not even the publicans so? Be ye, therefore, perfect, even as your Father which is in heaven is perfect.

11. Judge not, that ye be not judged. For with what judgment ye judge, ye shall be judged: and with what measure ye mete, it shall be measured to you again. And why beholdest thou the mote that is in thy brother's eye, but considerest not the beam that is in thine own eye?

12. Or how wilt thou say to thy brother, Let me pull out the mote out of thine eye; and, behold, a beam is in thine own eye? Thou hypocrite, first cast out the beam out of thine own eye; and then shalt thou see clearly to cast out the mote out of thy brother's eye.

13. Ask, and it shall be given you; seek, and ye shall find; knock, and it shall be opened unto you: for every one that asketh, receiveth; and he that seeketh, findeth; and to him that knocketh, it shall be opened. Or what man is there of you, whom if his son ask bread, will he give him a stone? Or if he ask a fish, will he give him a serpent?

14. If ye then, being evil, know how to give good gifts unto your children, how much more shall your Father which is in heaven give good things to them that ask him? Therefore all things whatsoever ye would

that men should do to you, do ye even so to them; for this is the law and the prophets.

15. Whosoever heareth these sayings of mine, and doeth them, I will liken him unto a wise man, which built his house upon a rock: and the rain descended, and the floods came, and the winds blew, and beat upon that house; and it fell not: for it was founded upon a rock.

16. And every one that heareth these sayings of mine, and doeth them not, shall be likened unto a foolish man, which built his house upon the sand: and the rain descended, and the floods came, and the winds blew, and beat upon that house; and it fell: and great was the fall of it.

17. And it came to pass, when Jesus had ended these sayings, the people were astonished at his doctrine: for he taught them as one having authority, and not as the scribes.

GARDINER SPRING

Observance of the Sabbath

The Sabbath lies at the foundation of all true morality. Morality flows from principle. Let the principles of moral obligation become relaxed, and the practice of morality will not long survive the overthrow. No man can preserve his own morals, no parent can preserve the morals of his children, without the impressions of religious obligation.

If you can induce a community to doubt the genuineness and authenticity of the Scriptures; to question the reality and obligations of religion; to hesitate, undeciding, whether there be any such thing as virtue or vice; whether there be an eternal state of retribution beyond the grave; or whether there exists any such being as God, you have broken down the barriers of moral virtue, and hoisted the flood-gates of immorality and crime. I need not say that when a people have once done this, they can no longer exist as a tranquil and happy people. Every bond that holds society together would be ruptured; fraud and treachery would take the place of confidence between man and man; the tribunals of justice would be scenes of bribery and injustice; avarice, perjury, ambition, and revenge

Gardiner Spring, "Observance of the Sabbath," Lesson 45, in *McGuffey's Sixth Eclectic Reader*, ed. William Holmes McGuffey (New York: American Book Company, 1879), 186–89.

would walk through the land, and render it more like the dwelling of savage beasts than the tranquil abode of civilized and Christianized men.

If there is an institution which opposes itself to this progress of human degeneracy, and throws a shield before the interests of moral virtue in our thoughtless and wayward world, it is the Sabbath. In the fearful struggle between virtue and vice, notwithstanding the powerful auxiliaries which wickedness finds in the bosoms of men, and in the seductions and influence of popular example, wherever the Sabbath has been suffered to live, the trembling interests of moral virtue have always been revered and sustained. One of the principal occupations of this day is to illustrate and enforce the great principles of sound morality. Where this sacred trust is preserved inviolate, you behold a nation convened one day in seven for the purpose of acquainting themselves with the best moral principles and precepts; and it can not be otherwise than that the authority of moral virtue, under such auspices, should be acknowledged and felt.

We may not, at once, perceive the effects which this weekly observance produces. Like most moral causes, it operates slowly; but it operates surely, and gradually weakens the power and breaks the yoke of profligacy and sin. No villain regards the Sabbath. No vicious family regards the Sabbath. No immoral community regards the Sabbath. The holy rest of this ever-memorable day is a barrier which is always broken down before men become giants in sin. Blackstone,[1] in his Commentaries on the Laws of England, remarks that "a corruption of morals usually follows a profanation of the Sabbath." It is an observation of Lord Chief-justice Hale,[2] that "of all the persons who were convicted of capital crimes, while he was on the bench, he found a few only who would not confess that they began their career of wickedness by a neglect of the duties of the Sabbath and vicious conduct on that day."

The prisons in our own land could probably tell us that they have scarcely a solitary tenant who had not broken over the restraints of the Sabbath before he was abandoned to crime. You may enact laws for the suppression of immorality, but the secret and silent power of the Sabbath constitutes a stronger shield to the vital interest of the community than any code of penal statutes that ever was enacted. The Sabbath is the keystone of the arch which sustains the temple of virtue, which, however defaced, will survive many a rude shock so long as the foundation remains firm.

[1]Sir William Blackstone (1723–1780), English jurist, professor of law, and author of the four-volume *Commentaries on the Laws of England.*

[2]Sir Matthew Hale (1609–1676), member of Parliament, chief justice of the King's Bench, and a noted legal scholar.

The observance of the Sabbath is also most influential in securing national prosperity. The God of Heaven has said, "Them that honor me I will honor." You will not often find a notorious Sabbath-breaker a permanently prosperous man; and a Sabbath-breaking community is never a happy or prosperous community. There is a multitude of unobserved influences which the Sabbath exerts upon the temporal welfare of men. It promotes the spirit of good order and harmony; it elevates the poor from want; it transforms squalid wretchedness; it imparts self-respect and elevation of character; it promotes softness and civility of manners; it brings together the rich and the poor upon one common level in the house of prayer; it purifies and strengthens the social affections, and makes the family circle the center of allurement and the source of instruction, comfort, and happiness. Like its own divine religion, "it has the promise of the life that now is and that which is to come," for men can not put themselves beyond the reach of hope and heaven so long as they treasure up this one command, "Remember the Sabbath-day, to keep it holy."

God's Goodness to Such as Fear Him

Fret not thyself because of evil-doers,
Neither be thou envious against the workers of iniquity;
For they shall soon be cut down like the grass,
And wither as the green herb.
Trust in the Lord, and do good;
So shalt thou dwell in the land, and verily thou shalt be fed.
Delight thyself also in the Lord,
And he shall give thee the desires of thine heart.
Commit thy way unto the Lord;
Trust also in him, and he shall bring it to pass.
And he shall bring forth thy righteousness as the light,
And thy judgment as the noonday.
Rest in the Lord, and wait patiently for him.

"God's Goodness to Such as Fear Him (from the Thirty-seventh Psalm)," Lesson 46, in *McGuffey's Sixth Eclectic Reader,* ed. William Holmes McGuffey (New York: American Book Company, 1879), 189–91.

Fret not thyself because of him who prospereth in his way,
Because of the man who bringeth wicked devices to pass.
Cease from anger, and forsake wrath:
Fret not thyself in any wise to do evil,
For evil-doers shall be cut off:
But those that wait upon the Lord, they shall inherit the earth.
For yet a little while, and the wicked shall not be;
Yea, thou shalt diligently consider his place, and it shall not be.
But the meek shall inherit the earth,
And shall delight themselves in the abundance of peace.

A little that a righteous man hath
Is better than the riches of many wicked;
For the arms of the wicked shall be broken,
But the Lord upholdeth the righteous.
The Lord knoweth the days of the upright,
And their inheritance shall be forever;
They shall not be ashamed in the evil time,
And in the days of famine they shall be satisfied.

But the wicked shall perish,
And the enemies of the Lord shall be as the fat of lambs;
They shall consume; into smoke shall they consume away,
The wicked borroweth, and payeth not again;
But the righteous sheweth mercy and giveth.
For such as be blessed of him shall inherit the earth.
The steps of a good man are ordered by the Lord,
And he delighteth in his way;
Though he fall, he shall not be utterly cast down;
For the Lord upholdeth him with his hand.

I have been young, and now am old,
Yet have I not seen the righteous forsaken,
Nor his seed begging bread.
He is ever merciful, and lendeth,
And his seed is blessed.

Depart from evil, and do good,
And dwell for evermore;
For the Lord loveth judgment,
And forsaketh not his saints:
They are preserved for ever:
But the seed of the wicked shall be cut off.

The righteous shall inherit the land,
And dwell therein for ever.
The mouth of the righteous speaketh wisdom,
And his tongue talketh of judgment;
The law of his God is in his heart;
None of his steps shall slide.
The wicked watcheth the righteous,
And seeketh to slay him.
The Lord will not leave him in his hand,
Nor condemn him when he is judged.

Wait on the Lord, and keep his way,
And he shall exalt thee to inherit the land;
When the wicked are cut off, thou shalt see it.
I have seen the wicked in great power,
And spreading himself like a green bay-tree;
Yet he passed away, and, lo, he was not;
Yea, I sought him, but he could not be found.

9

The Work Ethic

Work was not just a way to make a living in nineteenth-century America; it was the road to virtue. Not only did work add to the store of the world's goods, it also was closely tied to the ideal of manly independence. When a man worked, he refrained from other things such as drinking and gambling. The opposite of work, slothfulness, was particularly frightening to Victorians. But the ideal of work also created dilemmas for late nineteenth-century Americans. Work was associated with masculinity, yet increasing numbers of women were entering the workforce. In "Beautiful Hands," for example, the roughness of the working-class girl's hands is praised, yet her poverty makes her suspect. The system was supposed to reward hard labor with more than the daily grind. At the opposite end of the social spectrum, the lesson "Good-Will" asks what would happen if men's ambitions merely drove them to accumulate wealth without regard to doing good for others. Finally, "The Maniac" and "Song of the Shirt" express fears of the working world gone awry, of madness caused by overattention to one's tasks and of oppressive, factorylike labor, especially for women. The latter, of course, was already the reality for millions of Americans, even as the McGuffeys depicted America in bucolic, preindustrial hues. How do you think students reconciled the reality of the American workplace with the ideal presented by the McGuffey readers?

Henry, the Boot-Black

1. Henry was a kind, good boy. His father was dead, and his mother was very poor. He had a little sister about two years old.

2. He wanted to help his mother, for she could not always earn enough to buy food for her little family.

3. One day, a man gave him a dollar for finding a pocket-book which he had lost.

4. Henry might have kept all the money, for no one saw him when he found it. But his mother had taught him to be honest, and never to keep what did not belong to him.

5. With the dollar he bought a box, three brushes, and some blacking. He then went to the corner of the street, and said to every one whose boots did not look nice, "Black your boots, sir, please?"

6. He was so polite that gentlemen soon began to notice him, and to let him black their boots. The first day he brought home fifty cents, which he gave to his mother to buy food with.

7. When he gave her the money, she said, as she dropped a tear of joy, "You are a dear, good boy, Henry. I did not know how I could earn enough to buy bread with, but now I think we can manage to get along quite well."

8. Henry worked all the day, and went to school in the evening. He earned almost enough to support his mother and his little sister.

"Henry, the Boot-Black," Lesson 14, in *McGuffey's Second Eclectic Reader,* ed. William Holmes McGuffey (Chicago: American Book Company, 1879), 35–37.

The Fireside

1. One winter night, Mrs. Lord and her two little girls sat by a bright fire in their pleasant home. The girls were sewing, and their mother was busy at her knitting.

"The Fireside," Lesson 33, in *McGuffey's Second Eclectic Reader,* ed. William Holmes McGuffey (New York: American Book Company, 1879), 70–72.

2. At last, Katie finished her work, and, looking up, said, “Mother, I think the fire is brighter than usual. How I love to hear it crackle!”

3. “And I was about to say,” cried Mary, “that this is a better light than we had last night.”

4. “My dears,” said their mother, “it must be that you feel happier than usual to-night. Perhaps that is the reason why you think the fire better, and the light brighter.”

5. “But, mother,” said Mary, “I do not see why we are happier now than we were then; for last night cousin Jane was here, and we played ‘Puss in the corner’ and ‘Blind man’ until we all were tired.”

6. “I know! I know why!” said Katie. “It is because we have all been doing something useful to-night. We feel happy because we have been busy.”

7. “You are right, my dear,” said their mother. “I am glad you have both learned that there may be something more pleasant than play, and, at the same time, more instructive.”

Poor Davy

1. It was recess time at the village school. The bell had rung, and the children had run out into the bright sunshine, wild with laughter and fun.

2. All but poor Davy. He came out last and very slowly, but he did not laugh. He was in trouble, and the bright, golden sunlight did not make him glad.

3. He walked across the yard, and sat down on a stone behind the old maple. A little bird on the highest branch sang just to make him laugh.

4. But Davy did not notice it. He was thinking of the cruel words that had been said about his ragged clothes. The tears stole out of his eyes, and ran down his cheeks.

"Poor Davy," Lesson 65, in *McGuffey's Second Eclectic Reader,* ed. William Holmes McGuffey (New York: American Book Company, 1879), 144–48.

5. Poor Davy had no father, and his mother had to work hard to keep him at school.

6. That night, he went home by the path that led across the fields and through the woods. He still felt sad.

7. Davy did not wish to trouble his mother; so he lingered awhile among the trees, and at last threw himself on the green moss under them.

8. Just then his teacher came along. She saw who it was, and stopped, saying kindly, "What is the matter, Davy?"

9. He did not speak, but the tears began again to start.

10. "Won't you tell me? Perhaps I can help you."

11. Then he told her all his trouble. When he ended, she said, cheerily, "I have a plan, Davy, that I think will help you."

12. "Oh, what is it?" he said, sitting up with a look of hope, while a tear fell upon a blue violet.

13. "Well, how would you like to be a little flower merchant?"

14. "And earn money?" said Davy. "That would be jolly. But where shall I get my flowers?"

15. "Right in these woods, and in the fields," said his teacher. "Here are lovely blue violets, down by the brook are white ones, and among the rocks are ferns and mosses. Bring them all to my house, and I will help you arrange them."

16. So, day after day, Davy hunted the woods for the prettiest flowers, and the most dainty ferns and mosses. After his teacher had helped to arrange them, he took them to the city that was near, and sold them.

17. He soon earned money enough to buy new clothes. Now the sunshine and the bird's songs make him glad.

Beautiful Hands

1. "O Miss Roberts! what coarse-looking hands Mary Jessup has!" said Daisy Marvin, as she walked home from school with her teacher.

2. "In my opinion, Daisy, Mary's hands are the prettiest in the class."

"Beautiful Hands," Lesson 24, in *McGuffey's Third Eclectic Reader,* ed. William Holmes McGuffey (New York: American Book Company, 1879), 62–65.

3. "Why, Miss Roberts, they are as red and hard as they can be. How they would look if she were to try to play on a piano!" exclaimed Daisy.

4. Miss Roberts took Daisy's hands in hers, and said, "Your hands are very soft and white, Daisy—just the hands to look beautiful on a piano; yet they lack one beauty that Mary's hands have. Shall I tell you what the difference is?"

5. "Yes, please, Miss Roberts."

6. "Well, Daisy, Mary's hands are always busy. They wash dishes; they make fires; they hang out clothes, and help to wash them, too; they sweep, and dust, and sew; they are always trying to help her poor, hard-working mother.

7. "Besides, they wash and dress the children; they mend their toys and dress their dolls; yet, they find time to bathe the head of the little girl who is so sick in the next house to theirs.

8. "They are full of good deeds to every living thing. I have seen them

patting the tired horse and the lame dog in the street. They are always ready to help those who need help."

9. "I shall never think Mary's hands are ugly any more, Miss Roberts."

10. "I am glad to hear you say that, Daisy; and I must tell you that they are beautiful because they do their work gladly and cheerfully."

11. "O Miss Roberts! I feel so ashamed of myself, and so sorry," said Daisy, looking into her teacher's face with tearful eyes.

12. "Then, my dear, show your sorrow by deeds of kindness. The good alone are really beautiful."

Charlie and Rob

1. "Don't you hate splitting wood?" asked Charlie, as he sat down on a log to hinder Rob for a while.

2. "No, I rather like it. When I get hold of a tough old fellow, I say, 'See here, now, you think you're the stronger; and are going to beat me; so I'll split you up into kindling wood.' "

3. "Pshaw!" said Charlie, laughing; "and it's only a stick of wood."

4. "Yes; but you see I pretend it's a lesson, or a tough job of any kind, and it's nice to conquer it."

5. "I don't want to conquer such things; I don't care what becomes of them. I wish I was a man, and a rich one."

6. "Well, Charlie, if you live long enough you'll be a man, without wishing for it; and as for the rich part, I mean to be that myself."

7. "You do. How do you expect to get your money? By sawing wood?"

8. "May be—some of it; that's as good a way as any, so long as it lasts. I don't care how I get rich, you know, so that it's in an honest and useful way."

9. "I'd like to sleep over the next ten years, and wake up to find myself a young man with a splendid education and plenty of money."

10. "Humph! I am not sleepy—a night at a time is enough for me. I mean to work the next ten years. You see there are things that you've got to *work* out—you can't *sleep* them out."

11. "I hate work," said Charlie, "that is, such work as sawing and split-

"Charlie and Rob," Lesson 40, in *McGuffey's Third Eclectic Reader,* ed. William Holmes McGuffey (New York: American Book Company, 1879), 104–7.

ting wood, and doing chores. I'd like to do some big work, like being a clerk in a bank or something of that sort."

12. "Wood has to be sawed and split before it can be burned," said Rob. "I don't know but I'll be a clerk in a bank some time; I'm working towards it. I'm keeping father's accounts for him."

13. How Charlie laughed! "I should think that was a long way from being a bank clerk. I suppose your father sells two tables and six chairs, some days, doesn't he?"

14. "Sometimes more than that, and sometimes not so much," said Rob, in perfect good humor.

15. "I didn't say I was a bank clerk now. I said I was working towards it. Am I not nearer it by keeping a little bit of a book than I should be if I didn't keep any book at all?"

16. "Not a whit—such things *happen,*" said Charlie, as he started to go.

17. Now, which of these boys, do you think, grew up to be a rich and useful man, and which of them joined a party of tramps before he was thirty years old?

J. T. TROWBRIDGE

Good-Will

1. I suppose you all, my boys, are looking for some sort of success in life; it is right that you should; but what are your notions of success? To get rich as soon as possible, without regard to the means by which your wealth is acquired?

2. There is no true success in that: when you have gained millions, you may yet be poorer than when you had nothing; and it is that same reckless ambition which has brought many a bright and capable boy, not to great estate at last, but to miserable failure and disgrace; not to a palace, but to a prison.

3. Wealth rightly got and rightly used, rational enjoyment, power, fame,—these are all worthy objects of ambition; but they are not the highest objects, and you may acquire them all without achieving true success. But if, whatever you seek, you put good-will into all your actions, you are sure of the best success at last; for whatever else you gain or miss, you are building up a noble and beautiful character, which is not only the best of possessions in this world, but also is about all you can expect to take with you into the next.

4. I say, good-will in all your actions. You are not simply to be kind and helpful to others; but, whatever you do, give honest, earnest purpose

J. T. Trowbridge, "Good-Will," Lesson 57, in *McGuffey's Fourth Eclectic Reader,* ed. William Holmes McGuffey (New York: American Book Company, 1879), 153–56.

to it. Thomas is put by his parents to learn a business. But Thomas does not like to apply himself very closely. "What's the use?" he says. "I'm not paid much, and I'm not going to work much. I'll get along just as easily as I can, and have as good times as I can."

5. So he shirks his tasks; and instead of thinking about his employer's interests, or his own self-improvement, gives his mind to trifles—often to evil things, which in their ruinous effects upon his life are not trifles. As soon as he is free from his daily duties, he is off with his companions, having what they call a good time; his heart is with them even while his hands are employed in the shop or store.

6. He does nothing thoroughly well,—not at all for want of talent, but solely for lack of good-will. He is not preparing himself to be one of those efficient clerks or workmen who are always in demand, and who receive the highest wages.

7. There is a class of people who are the pest of every community, workmen who do not know their trade, men of business ignorant of the first principles of business. They can never be relied upon to do well any thing they undertake. They are always making blunders which other people have to suffer for, and which react upon themselves. They are always getting out of employment, and failing in business.

8. To make up for what they lack in knowledge and thoroughness, they often resort to trick and fraud, and become not merely contemptible but criminal. Thomas is preparing himself to be one of this class. You can not, boys, expect to raise a good crop from evil seed.

9. By Thomas's side works another boy, whom we will call James,—a lad of only ordinary capacity, very likely. If Thomas and all the other boys did their best, there would be but small chance for James ever to become eminent. But he has something better than talent: he brings good-will to his work. Whatever he learns, he learns so well that it becomes a part of himself.

10. His employers find that they can depend upon him. Customers soon learn to like and trust him. By diligence, self-culture, good habits, cheerful and kindly conduct, he is laying the foundation of a generous manhood and a genuine success.

11. In short, boys, by slighting your tasks you hurt yourself more than you wrong your employer. By honest service you benefit yourself more than you help him. If you were aiming at mere worldly advancement only, I should still say that good-will was the very best investment you could make in business.

12. By cheating a customer, you gain only a temporary and unreal

advantage. By serving him with right good-will,—doing by him as you would be done by,—you not only secure his confidence but also his good-will in return. But this is a sordid consideration compared with the inward satisfaction, the glow and expansion of soul which attend a good action done for itself alone. If I were to sum up all I have to say to you in one last word of love and counsel, that one word should be—Good-will.

The Maniac

1. A gentleman who had traveled in Europe, relates that he one day visited the hospital of Berlin, where he saw a man whose exterior was very striking. His figure, tall and commanding, was bending with age, but more with sorrow; the few scattered hairs which remained on his temples were white almost as the driven snow, and the deepest melancholy was depicted in his countenance.

2. On inquiring who he was and what brought him there, he started, as if from sleep, and, after looking around him, began with slow and measured steps to stride the hall, repeating in a low but audible voice, "Once one is two; once one is two."

3. Now and then he would stop, and remain with his arms folded on his breast as if in contemplation, for some minutes; then again resuming his walk, he continued to repeat, "Once one is two; once one is two." His story, as our traveler understood it, was as follows.

4. Conrad Lange, collector of the revenues of the city of Berlin, had long been known as a man whom nothing could divert from the paths of honesty. Scrupulously exact in all his dealings, and assiduous in the discharge of all his duties, he had acquired the good-will and esteem of all who knew him, and the confidence of the minister of finance, whose duty it is to inspect the accounts of all officers connected with the revenue.

5. On casting up his accounts at the close of a particular year, he found a deficit of ten thousand ducats. Alarmed at this discovery, he went to the minister, presented his accounts, and informed him that he did not know

"The Maniac," Lesson 9, in *McGuffey's Fifth Eclectic Reader,* ed. William Holmes McGuffey (New York: American Book Company, 1879), 60–61.

how it had arisen, and that he had been robbed by some person bent on his ruin.

6. The minister received his accounts, but thinking it a duty to secure a person who might probably be a defaulter, he caused him to be arrested, and put his accounts into the hands of one of his secretaries for inspection, who returned them the day after with the information that the deficiency arose from a miscalculation; that in multiplying, Mr. Lange had said, *once one is two,* instead of once one is *one.*

7. The poor man was immediately released from confinement, his accounts returned, and the mistake pointed out. During his imprisonment, which lasted two days, he had neither eaten, drank, nor taken any repose; and when he appeared, his countenance was as pale as death. On receiving his accounts, he was a long time silent; then suddenly awaking, as if from a trance, he repeated, "Once one is two."

8. He appeared to be entirely insensible of his situation; would neither eat nor drink, unless solicited; and took notice of nothing that passed around him. While repeating his accustomed phrase, if any one corrected him by saying, "Once one is *one,"* his attention was arrested for a moment, and he said, "Ah, right, once one *is* one;" and then resuming his walk, he continued to repeat, "Once one is two." He died shortly after the traveler left Berlin.

9. This affecting story, whether true or untrue, obviously abounds with lessons of instruction. Alas! how easily is the human mind thrown off its balance; especially when it is stayed on this world only, and has no experimental knowledge of the meaning of the injunction of Scripture, to cast all our cares upon Him who careth for us, and who heareth even the young ravens when they cry.

Behind Time

1. A railroad train was rushing along at almost lightning speed. A curve was just ahead, beyond which was a station where two trains usually met. The conductor was late,—so late that the period during which the up-train was to wait had nearly elapsed; but he hoped yet to pass the

"Behind Time," Lesson 49, in *McGuffey's Fifth Eclectic Reader,* ed. William Holmes McGuffey (New York: American Book Company, 1879), 161–63.

curve safely. Suddenly a locomotive dashed into sight right ahead. In an instant there was a collision. A shriek, a shock, and fifty souls were in eternity; and all because an engineer had been behind time.

2. A great battle was going on. Column after column had been precipitated for eight hours on the enemy posted along the ridge of a hill. The summer sun was sinking in the west; re-enforcements for the obstinate defenders were already in sight; it was necessary to carry the position with one final charge, or every thing would be lost.

3. A powerful corps had been summoned from across the country, and if it came up in season all would yet be well. The great conqueror, confident in its arrival, formed his reserve into an attacking column, and ordered them to charge the enemy. The whole world knows the result. Grouchy failed to appear; the imperial guard was beaten back; and Waterloo was lost. Napoleon died a prisoner at St. Helena because one of his marshals was behind time.[1]

4. A leading firm in commercial circles had long struggled against bankruptcy. As it had large sums of money in California, it expected remittances by a certain day, and if they arrived, its credit, its honor, and its future prosperity would be preserved. But week after week elapsed without bringing the gold. At last came the fatal day on which the firm had bills maturing to large amounts. The steamer was telegraphed at daybreak; but it was found, on inquiry, that she brought no funds, and the house failed. The next arrival brought nearly half a million to the insolvents, but it was too late; they were ruined because their agent, in remitting, had been behind time.

5. A condemned man was led out for execution. He had taken human life, but under circumstances of the greatest provocation, and public sympathy was active in his behalf. Thousands had signed petitions for a reprieve; a favorable answer had been expected the night before, and though it had not come, even the sheriff felt confident that it would yet arrive. Thus the morning passed without the appearance of the messenger.

6. The last moment was up. The prisoner took his place, the cap was drawn over his eyes, the bolt was drawn, and a lifeless body swung revolving in the wind. Just at that moment a horseman came into sight, galloping down hill, his steed covered with foam. He carried a packet in his right

[1]As emperor, Napoleon Bonaparte (1769–1821) extended the French Empire from Spain to Poland in the early nineteenth century. His army was crushed and his empire crumbled after a decisive victory by English and Prussian forces at the Belgian town of Waterloo.

hand, which he waved frantically to the crowd. He was the express rider with the reprieve; but he came too late. A comparatively innocent man had died an ignominious death because a watch had been five minutes too late, making its bearer arrive behind time.

7. It is continually so in life. The best laid plans, the most important affairs, the fortunes of individuals, the weal of nations, honor, happiness, life itself, are daily sacrificed, because somebody is "behind time." There are men who always fail in whatever they undertake, simply because they are "behind time." There are others who put off reformation year after year, till death seizes them, and they perish unrepentant, because forever "behind time."

THOMAS HOOD

Song of the Shirt

With fingers weary and worn,
With eyelids heavy and red,
A woman sat, in unwomanly rags,
Plying her needle and thread:
Stitch! stitch! stitch!
In poverty, hunger, and dirt,
And still with a voice of dolorous pitch,
She sang the "Song of the Shirt!"

"Work! work! work!
While the cock is crowing aloof!
And work! work! work!
Till the stars shine through the roof!
It is oh to be a slave
Along with the barbarous Turk,
Where woman has never a soul to save,
If this is Christian work!

"Work! work! work!
Till the brain begins to swim;

Thomas Hood, "Song of the Shirt," Lesson 73, in *McGuffey's Sixth Eclectic Reader,* ed. William Holmes McGuffey (New York: American Book Company, 1879), pp. 266–69.

Work! work! work!
Till the eyes are heavy and dim!
Seam, and gusset, and band,
Band, and gusset, and seam,
Till over the buttons I fall asleep,
And sew them on in a dream!

"O men, with sisters dear!
O men, with mothers and wives!
It is not linen you're wearing out,
But human creatures' lives!
Stitch! stitch! stitch!
In poverty, hunger, and dirt,—
Sewing at once, with a double thread,
A shroud as well as a shirt.

"But why do I talk of Death?
That Phantom of grisly bone,
I hardly fear his terrible shape,
It seems so like my own;
It seems so like my own,
Because of the fasts I keep;
O God! that bread should be so dear,
And flesh and blood so cheap!

"Work! work! work!
My labor never flags;
And what are its wages? A bed of straw,
A crust of bread—and rags,
That shattered roof—and this naked floor—
A table—a broken chair—
And a wall so blank, my shadow I thank
For sometimes falling there.

"Work! work! work!
From weary chime to chime!
Work! work! work!
As prisoners work for crime!
Band, and gusset, and seam,
Seam, and gusset, and band,
Till the heart is sick, and the brain benumbed,
As well as the weary hand.

"Work! work! work!
In the dull December light,
And work! work! work!
When the weather is warm and bright;
While underneath the eaves
The brooding swallows cling,
As if to show me their sunny backs,
And twit me with the spring.

"Oh but to breathe the breath
Of the cowslip and primrose sweet!
With the sky above my head,
And the grass beneath my feet!
For only one short hour
To feel as I used to feel,
Before I knew the woes of want,
And the walk that costs a meal!

"Oh but for one short hour,—
A respite, however brief!
No blessèd leisure for love or hope,
But only time for grief!
A little weeping would ease my heart,
But in their briny bed
My tears must stop, for every drop
Hinders needle and thread."

With fingers weary and worn,
With eyelids heavy and red,
A woman sat, in unwomanly rags,
Plying her needle and thread:
Stitch! stitch! stitch!
In poverty, hunger, and dirt,
And still with a voice of dolorous pitch—
Would that its tone could reach the rich!—
She sang this "Song of the Shirt."

10
Citizenship

How do democratic societies ensure that individuals act not only on their self-interest, but also with the good of the whole in mind? What sources of authority engender a sense of community and of citizenship? The McGuffey readers implicitly offered some solutions to these problems. In "The Young Witness," God's commandment against bearing false witness assures accurate testimony in court; in "Rebellion in Massachusetts State-Prison," the moral force of Commander Wainright's personality and the righteousness of his cause lead to a good outcome; in "The Best Kind of Revenge," simple truth overcomes the ill effects of libel. As Alexis de Tocqueville pointed out in the 1830s, democratic societies' tendencies to set individuals apart were countered by what he called "voluntary associations." Citizens acting in concert for specific purposes—to build a road, to start a temperance society, or to reform the public schools—gave people common interests and kept them from going their separate ways. In the following selections, what sorts of social glue do the McGuffeys suggest to bind people together?

S. H. HAMMOND
The Young Witness

1. A little girl nine years of age was brought into court, and offered as a witness against a prisoner who was on trial for a crime committed in her father's house.

2. "Now, Emily," said the counsel for the prisoner, "I wish to know if you understand the nature of an oath?"

S. H. Hammond, "The Young Witness," Lesson 74, in *McGuffey's Fourth Eclectic Reader,* ed. William Holmes McGuffey (New York: American Book Company, 1879), 207–10.

3. "I don't know what you mean," was the simple answer.

4. "Your Honor," said the counsel, addressing the judge, "it is evident that this witness should be rejected. She does not understand the nature of an oath."

5. "Let us see," said the judge. "Come here, my daughter."

6. Assured by the kind tone and manner of the judge, the child stepped toward him, and looked confidingly in his face, with a calm, clear eye, and in a manner so artless and frank that it went straight to the heart.

7. "Did you ever take an oath?" inquired the judge.

8. The little girl stepped back with a look of horror; and the red blood rose and spread in a blush all over her face and neck, as she answered, "No, sir." She thought he intended to ask if she had ever used profane language.

9. "I do not mean that," said the judge, who saw her mistake; "I mean were you ever a witness?"

10. "No, sir; I never was in court before," was the answer.

11. He handed her the Bible open. "Do you know that book, my daughter?"

12. She looked at it and answered, "Yes, sir; it is the Bible."

13. "Do you ever read in it?" he asked.

14. "Yes, sir; every evening."

15. "Can you tell me what the Bible is?" inquired the judge.

16. "It is the word of the great God," she answered.

17. "Well," said the judge, "place your hand upon this Bible, and listen to what I say;" and he repeated slowly and solemnly the following oath: "Do you swear that in the evidence which you shall give in this case, you will tell the truth, and nothing but the truth; and that you will ask God to help you?"

18. "I do," she replied.

19. "Now," said the judge, "you have been sworn as a witness; will you tell me what will befall you if you do not tell the truth?"

20. "I shall be shut up in the state-prison," answered the child.

21. "Any thing else?" asked the judge.

22. "I shall never go to heaven," she replied.

23. "How do you know this?" asked the judge again.

24. The child took the Bible, turned rapidly to the chapter containing the commandments, and, pointing to the one which reads, "Thou shalt not bear false witness against thy neighbor," said, "I learned that before I could read."

25. "Has any one talked with you about being a witness in court here against this man?" inquired the judge.

26. "Yes, sir," she replied, "my mother heard they wanted me to be a witness; and last night she called me to her room, and asked me to tell her the Ten Commandments; and then we kneeled down together, and she prayed that I might understand how wicked it was to bear false witness against my neighbor, and that God would help me, a little child, to tell the truth as it was before him.

27. "And when I came up here with father, she kissed me, and told me to remember the Ninth Commandment, and that God would hear every word that I said."

28. "Do you believe this?" asked the judge, while a tear glistened in his eye, and his lip quivered with emotion.

29. "Yes, sir," said the child, with a voice and manner which showed that her conviction of the truth was perfect.

30. "God bless you, my child," said the judge, "you have a good mother. The witness is competent," he continued. "Were I on trial for my life, and innocent of the charge against me, I would pray God for such a witness as this. Let her be examined."

31. She told her story with the simplicity of a child, as she was; but her voice and manner carried conviction of her truthfulness to every heart.

32. The lawyers asked her many perplexing questions, but she did not vary in the least from her first statement.

33. The truth, as spoken by a little child, was sublime. Falsehood and perjury had preceded her testimony; but before her testimony, falsehood was scattered like chaff.

34. The little child, for whom a mother had prayed for strength to be given her to speak the truth as it was before God, broke the cunning device of matured villainy to pieces, like a potter's vessel. The strength that her mother prayed for was given her; and the sublime and terrible simplicity,—terrible to the prisoner and his associates,—was like a revelation from God himself.

J. T. BUCKINGHAM

Rebellion in Massachusetts State-Prison

1. A more impressive exhibition of moral courage, opposed to the wildest ferocity under the most appalling circumstances, was never seen than that which was witnessed by the officers of our state-prison, in the rebellion which occurred some years since.

2. Three convicts had been sentenced, under the rules of the prison, to be whipped in the yard, and, by some effort of one of the other prisoners, a door had been opened at midday communicating with the great dining-hall and, through the warden's lodge, with the street.

3. The dining-hall was long, dark, and damp, from its situation near the surface of the ground; and in this all the prisoners assembled, with clubs and such other tools as they could seize in passing through the workshops.

4. Knives, hammers, and chisels, with every variety of such weapons, were in the hands of the ferocious spirits, who are drawn away from their encroachments on society, forming a congregation of strength, vileness, and talent that can hardly be equaled on earth, even among the famed brigands of Italy.

5. Men of all ages and characters, guilty of every variety of infamous crime, dressed in the motley and peculiar garb of the institution, and displaying the wild and demoniac appearance that always pertains to imprisoned wretches, were gathered together for the single purpose of preventing the punishment which was to be inflicted on the morrow upon their comrades.

6. The warden, the surgeon, and some other officers of the prison were there at the time, and were alarmed at the consequences likely to ensue from the conflict necessary to restore order. They huddled together, and could scarcely be said to consult, as the stoutest among them lost all presence of mind in overwhelming fear. The news rapidly spread through the town, and a subordinate officer, of the most mild and kind disposition, hurried to the scene, and came calm and collected into the midst of the officers. The most equable-tempered and the mildest man in the government was in this hour of peril the firmest.

7. He instantly dispatched a request to Major Wainright, commander

---

J. T. Buckingham, "Rebellion in Massachusetts State-Prison," Lesson 41, in *McGuffey's Fifth Eclectic Reader,* ed. William Holmes McGuffey (New York: American Book Company, 1879), 138–42.

of the marines stationed at the Navy Yard, for assistance, and declared his purpose to enter into the hall and try the force of firm demeanor and persuasion upon the enraged multitude.

8. All his brethren exclaimed against an attempt so full of hazard, but in vain. They offered him arms, a sword and pistols, but he refused them, and said that he had no fear, and, in case of danger, arms would do him no service; and alone, with only a little rattan, which was his usual walking-stick, he advanced into the hall to hold parley with the selected, congregated, and enraged villains of the whole commonwealth.

9. He demanded their purpose in thus coming together with arms, in violation of the prison laws. They replied that they were determined to obtain the remission of the punishment of their three comrades. He said it was impossible; the rules of the prison must be obeyed, and they must submit.

10. At the hint of submission they drew a little nearer together, prepared their weapons for service, and, as they were dimly seen in the further end of the hall by those who observed from the gratings that opened up to the day, a more appalling sight can not be conceived, nor one of more moral grandeur, than that of the single man standing within their grasp, and exposed to be torn limb from limb instantly if a word or look should add to the already intense excitement.

11. That excitement, too, was of a most dangerous kind. It broke not forth in noise and imprecations, but was seen only in the dark looks and the strained nerves that showed a deep determination. The officer expostulated. He reminded them of the hopelessness of escape; that the town was alarmed, and that the government of the prison would submit to nothing but unconditional surrender. He said that all those who would go quietly away should be forgiven for this offense; but, that if every prisoner were killed in the contest, power enough would be obtained to enforce the regulations of the prison.

12. They replied that they expected that some would be killed,—that death would be better than such imprisonment; and, with that look and tone which bespeak an indomitable purpose, they declared that not a man should leave the hall alive till the flogging was remitted. At this period of the discussion their evil passions seemed to be more inflamed, and one or two offered to destroy the officer, who still stood firmer and with a more temperate pulse than did his friends, who saw from above, but could not avert, the danger that threatened him.

13. Just at this moment, and in about fifteen minutes from the commencement of the tumult, the officer saw the feet of the marines, on whose presence alone he relied for succor, filing by the small upper lights. Without any apparent anxiety, he had repeatedly turned his atten-

tion to their approach; and now he knew that it was his only time to escape, before the conflict became, as was expected, one of the most dark and dreadful in the world.

14. He stepped slowly backward, still urging them to depart before the officers were driven to use the last resort of fire-arms. When within three or four feet of the door, it was opened, and closed instantly again as he sprang through, and was thus unexpectedly restored to his friends.

15. Major Wainright was requested to order his men to fire down upon the convicts through the little windows, first with powder and then with ball, till they were willing to retreat; but he took a wiser as well as a bolder course, relying upon the effect which firm determination would have upon men so critically situated. He ordered the door to be again opened, and marched in at the head of twenty or thirty men, who filed through the passage, and formed at the end of the hall opposite to the crowd of criminals huddled together at the other.

16. He stated that he was empowered to quell the rebellion, that he wished to avoid shedding blood, but that he would not quit that hall alive till every convict had returned to his duty. They seemed balancing the strength of the two parties, and replied that some of them were ready to die, and only waited for an attack to see which was the more powerful; swearing that they would fight to the last, unless the punishment was remitted, for they would not submit to any such punishment in the prison. Major Wainright ordered his marines to load their pieces, and, that they might not be suspected of trifling, each man was made to hold up to view the bullet which he afterward put in his gun.

17. This only caused a growl of determination, and no one blenched or seemed disposed to shrink from the foremost exposure. They knew that their number would enable them to bear down and destroy the handful of marines after the first discharge, and before their pieces could be reloaded. Again they were ordered to retire; but they answered with more ferocity than ever. The marines were ordered to take their aim so as to be sure and kill as many as possible. Their guns were presented, but not a prisoner stirred, except to grasp more firmly his weapon.

18. Still desirous to avoid such a tremendous slaughter as must have followed the discharge of a single gun, Major Wainright advanced a step or two, and spoke even more firmly than before, urging them to depart. Again, and while looking directly into the muzzles of the guns which they had seen loaded with ball, they declared their intention "to fight it out." This intrepid officer then took out his watch, and told his men to hold their pieces aimed at the convicts, but not to fire till they had orders; then, turn-

ing to the prisoners, he said: "You must leave this hall; I give you three minutes to decide; if at the end of that time a man remains, he shall be shot dead."

19. No situation of greater interest than this can be conceived. At one end of the hall, a fearful multitude of the most desperate and powerful men in existence, waiting for the assault; at the other, a little band of disciplined men, waiting with arms presented, and ready, upon the least motion or sign, to begin the carnage; and their tall and imposing commander, holding up his watch to count the lapse of three minutes, given as the reprieve to the lives of hundreds. No poet or painter can conceive a spectacle of more dark and terrible sublimity; no human heart can conceive a situation of more appalling suspense.

20. For two minutes not a person nor a muscle moved; not a sound was heard in the unwonted stillness of the prison, except the labored breathings of the infuriated wretches, as they began to pant between fear and revenge: at the expiration of two minutes, during which they had faced the ministers of death with unblenching eyes, two or three of those in the rear, and nearest the further entrance, went slowly out; a few more followed the example, dropping out quietly and deliberately; and before half of the last minute was gone, every man was struck by the panic, and crowded for an exit, and the hall was cleared as if by magic.

21. Thus the steady firmness of moral force and the strong effect of determination, acting deliberately, awed the most savage men, and suppressed a scene of carnage, which would have instantly followed the least precipitancy or exertion of physical force.

The Best Kind of Revenge

1. Some years ago a warehouseman in Manchester, England, published a scurrilous pamphlet, in which he endeavored to hold up the house of Grant Brothers to ridicule. William Grant remarked upon the occurrence that the man would live to repent of what he had done; and this was conveyed by some tale-bearer to the libeler, who said, "Oh, I suppose he thinks I shall some time or other be in his debt; but I will take good care of that." It happens, however, that a man in business can not

"The Best Kind of Revenge," Lesson 85, in *McGuffey's Fifth Eclectic Reader,* ed. William Holmes McGuffey (New York: American Book Company, 1879), 266–68.

always choose who shall be his creditors. The pamphleteer became a bankrupt, and the brothers held an acceptance of his which had been indorsed to them by the drawer, who had also become a bankrupt.

2. The wantonly libeled men had thus become creditors of the libeler! They now had it in their power to make him repent of his audacity. He could not obtain his certificate without their signature, and without it he could not enter into business again. He had obtained the number of signatures required by the bankrupt law except one. It seemed folly to hope that the firm of "the brothers" would supply the deficiency. What! they who had cruelly been made the laughing-stock of the public, forget the wrong and favor the wrong-doer? He despaired. But the claims of a wife and children forced him at last to make the application. Humbled by misery, he presented himself at the counting-house of the wronged.

3. Mr. William Grant was there alone, and his first words to the delinquent were, "Shut the door, sir!" sternly uttered. The door was shut, and the libeler stood trembling before the libeled. He told his tale and produced his certificate, which was instantly clutched by the injured merchant. "You wrote a pamphlet against us once!" exclaimed Mr. Grant. The suppliant expected to see his parchment thrown into the fire. But this was not its destination. Mr. Grant took a pen, and writing something upon the document, handed it back to the bankrupt. He, poor wretch, expected to see "rogue, scoundrel, libeler," inscribed; but there was, in fair round characters, the signature of the firm.

4. "We make it a rule," said Mr. Grant, "Never to refuse signing the certificate of an honest tradesman, and we have never heard that you were any thing else." The tears started into the poor man's eyes. "Ah," said Mr. Grant, "My saying was true! I said you would live to repent writing that pamphlet. I did not mean it as a threat. I only meant that some day you would know us better, and be sorry you had tried to injure us. I see you repent of it now." "I do, I do!" said the grateful man; "I bitterly repent it." "Well, well, my dear fellow, you know us now. How do you get on? What are you going to do?" The poor man stated he had friends who could assist him when his certificate was obtained. "But how are you off in the meantime?"

5. And the answer was, that, having given up every farthing to his creditors, he had been compelled to stint his family of even common necessaries, that he might be enabled to pay the cost of his certificate. "My dear fellow, this will not do; your family must not suffer. Be kind enough to take this ten-pound note to your wife from me. There, there, my dear fellow! Nay, do not cry; it will all be well with you yet. Keep up your spirits, set to work like a man, and you will raise your head among us yet." The overpowered man endeavored in vain to express his thanks; the swelling

in his throat forbade words. He put his handkerchief to his face and went out of the door, crying like a child.

WILLIAM ELLERY CHANNING

Religion the Only Basis of Society

1. Religion is a social concern; for it operates powerfully on society, contributing in various ways to its stability and prosperity. Religion is not merely a private affair; the community is deeply interested in its diffusion; for it is the best support of the virtues and principles, on which the social order rests. Pure and undefiled religion is, to do good; and it follows, very plainly, that if God be the Author and Friend of society, then, the recognition of him must enforce all social duty, and enlightened piety must give its whole strength to public order.

2. Few men suspect, perhaps no man comprehends, the extent of the support given by religion to every virtue. No man, perhaps, is aware, how much our moral and social sentiments are fed from this fountain; how powerless conscience would become without the belief of a God; how palsied would be human benevolence, were there not the sense of a higher benevolence to quicken and sustain it; how suddenly the whole social fabric would quake, and with what a fearful crash it would sink into hopeless ruin, were the ideas of a Supreme Being, of accountableness and of a future life to be utterly erased from every mind.

3. And, let men thoroughly believe that they are the work and sport of chance; that no superior intelligence concerns itself with human affairs; that all their improvements perish forever at death; that the weak have no guardian, and the injured no avenger; that there is no recompense for sacrifices to uprightness and the public good; that an oath is unheard in heaven; that secret crimes have no witness but the perpetrator; that human existence has no purpose, and human virtue no unfailing friend; that this brief life is every thing to us, and death is total, everlasting extinction; once let them *thoroughly* abandon religion, and who can conceive or describe the extent of the desolation which would follow?

William Ellery Channing, "Religion the Only Basis of Society," Lesson 93, in *McGuffey's Fifth Eclectic Reader,* ed. William Holmes McGuffey (New York: American Book Company, 1879), 284–86.

4. We hope, perhaps, that human laws and natural sympathy would hold society together. As reasonably might we believe, that were the sun quenched in the heavens, *our* torches would illuminate, and *our* fires quicken and fertilize the creation. What is there in human nature to awaken respect and tenderness, if man is the unprotected insect of a day? And what is he more, if atheism be true?

5. Erase all thought and fear of God from a community, and selfishness and sensuality would absorb the whole man. Appetite, knowing no restraint, and suffering, having no solace or hope, would trample in scorn on the restraints of human laws. Virtue, duty, principle, would be mocked and spurned as unmeaning sounds. A sordid self-interest would supplant every feeling; and man would become, in fact, what the theory in atheism declares him to be,—*a companion for brutes.*

THOMAS JEFFERSON

Political Toleration

During the contest of opinion through which we have passed, the animation of discussions and of exertions has sometimes worn an aspect which might impose on strangers, unused to think freely and to speak and to write what they think; but this being now decided by the voice of the nation, announced according to the rules of the constitution, all will, of course, arrange themselves under the will of the law, and unite in common efforts for the common good.

All, too, will bear in mind this sacred principle, that, though the will of the majority is, in all cases, to prevail, that will, to be rightful, must be reasonable; that the minority possess their equal rights, which equal laws must protect, and to violate which would be oppression. Let us then, fellow-citizens, unite with one heart and one mind.

Let us restore to social intercourse that harmony and affection, without which liberty, and even life itself, are but dreary things; and let us reflect, that, having banished from our land that religious intolerance under which mankind so long bled and suffered, we have gained little if

Thomas Jefferson, "Political Toleration," Lesson 67, in *McGuffey's Sixth Eclectic Reader,* ed. William Holmes McGuffey (New York: American Book Company, 1879), 253–55.

we countenance a political intolerance as despotic, as wicked, and capable of as bitter and bloody persecutions.

During the throes and convulsions of the ancient world; during the agonizing spasms of infuriated man, seeking, through blood and slaughter, his long-lost liberty; it was not wonderful that the agitation of the billows should reach even this distant and peaceful shore; that this should be more felt and feared by some, and less by others, and should divide opinions as to measures of safety.

But every difference of opinion is not a difference of principle. We have called by different names brethren of the same principle. We are all Republicans; we are all Federalists. If there be any among us who would wish to dissolve this Union, or to change its republican form, let them stand undisturbed as monuments of the safety with which error of opinion may be tolerated when reason is left free to combat it.

I know, indeed, that some honest men fear that a republican government can not be strong; that this government is not strong enough. But would the honest patriot, in the full tide of successful experiment, abandon a government which has so far kept us free and firm, on the theoretic and visionary fear that this government, the world's best hope, may, by possibility, want energy to preserve itself? I trust not; I believe this, on the contrary, the strongest government on earth.

I believe it to be the only one where every man, at the call of the law, would fly to the standard of the law, and would meet invasions of the public order as his own personal concern. Sometimes it is said that man can not be trusted with the government of himself. Can he, then, be trusted with the government of others, or have we found angels, in the form of kings, to govern him? Let history answer this question. Let us, then, with courage and confidence, pursue our own federal and republican principles; our attachment to union and representative government.

HORACE GREELEY

Labor

Every child should be trained to dexterity in some useful branch of productive industry, not in order that he shall certainly follow that pursuit, but that he may at all events be able to do so in case he shall fail in the more intellectual or artificial calling which he may prefer to it. Let him seek to be a doctor, lawyer, preacher, poet, if he will; but let him not stake his all on success in that pursuit, but have a second line to fall back upon if driven from his first. Let him be so reared and trained that he may enter, if he will, upon some intellectual calling in the sustaining consciousness that he need not debase himself, nor do violence to his convictions, in order to achieve success therein, since he can live and thrive in another (if you choose, humbler) vocation, if driven from that of his choice. This buttress to integrity, this assurance of self-respect, is to be found in a universal training to efficiency in Productive Labor.

The world is full of misdirection and waste; but all the calamities and losses endured by mankind through frost, drouth, blight, hail, fires, earthquakes, inundations, are as nothing to those habitually suffered by them through human idleness and inefficiency, mainly caused (or excused) by lack of industrial training. It is quite within the truth to estimate that one tenth of our people, in the average, are habitually idle because (as they say) they can find no employment. They look for work where it can not be had. They seem to be, or they are, unable to do such as abundantly confronts and solicits them. Suppose these to average but one million able-bodied persons, and that their work is worth but one dollar each per day; our loss by involuntary idleness can not be less than $300,000,000 per annum. I judge that it is actually $500,000,000. Many who stand waiting to be hired could earn from two to five dollars per day had they been properly trained to work. "There is plenty of room higher up," said Daniel Webster, in response to an inquiry as to the prospects of a young man just entering upon the practice of law; and there is never a dearth of employment for men or women of signal capacity or skill. In this city, ten thousand women are always doing needle-work for less than fifty cents per day, finding themselves; yet twice their number of capable, skillful seamstresses could find steady employment and good living in wealthy

---

Horace Greeley, "Labor," Lesson 114, in *McGuffey's Sixth Eclectic Reader,* ed. William Holmes McGuffey (New York: American Book Company, 1879), 398–400.

families at not less than one dollar per day over and above board and lodging. He who is a good blacksmith, a fair mill-wright, a tolerable wagon-maker, and can chop timber, make fence, and manage a small farm if required, is always sure of work and fair recompense; while he or she who can keep books or teach music fairly, but knows how to do nothing else, is in constant danger of falling into involuntary idleness and consequent beggary. It is a broad, general truth, that no boy was ever yet inured to daily, systematic, productive labor in field or shop throughout the latter half of his minority, who did not prove a useful man, and was not able to find work whenever he wished it.

Yet to the ample and constant employment of a whole community one prerequisite is indispensable,—that a variety of pursuits shall have been created or naturalized therein. A people who have but a single source of profit are uniformly poor, not because that vocation is necessarily ill-chosen, but because no single calling can employ and reward the varied capacities of male and female, old and young, robust and feeble. Thus a lumbering or fishing region with us is apt to have a large proportion of needy inhabitants; and the same is true of a region exclusively devoted to cotton-growing or gold-mining. A diversity of pursuits is indispensable to general activity and enduring prosperity.

Sixty or seventy years ago, what was then the District, and is now the State, of Maine, was a proverb in New England for the poverty of its people, mainly because they were so largely engaged in timber-cutting. The great grain-growing, wheat-exporting districts of the Russian empire have a poor and rude people for a like reason. Thus the industry of Massachusetts is immensely more productive per head than that of North Carolina, or even that of Indiana, as it will cease to be whenever manufactures shall have been diffused over our whole country, as they must and will be. In Massachusetts half the women and nearly half the children add by their daily labor to the aggregate of realized wealth; in North Carolina and in Indiana little wealth is produced save by the labor of men, including boys of fifteen or upward. When this disparity shall have ceased, its consequence will also disappear.

11
History

Few school children during the nineteenth century took classes in history. In fact, history as a profession did not exist when the 1879 McGuffey edition was published. No graduate school yet trained people to assess primary documents and compose historical narratives. Amateur historians, many of them widely read and brilliant individuals, were keepers of the nation's past and writers of its story. The purpose of history, they believed, was to reveal the working out of God's plan through time or to show the inevitable spread of grand ideas such as democracy and equality. Thus, the lesson on "North American Indians" combined nostalgia over the passing of Native Americans with smug satisfaction that they perished before a superior civilization. Historical figures like Christopher Columbus, George Washington, or the Puritan "fathers" were models to be emulated. Stirring speeches like Patrick Henry's confirmed that American history represented the unfolding of progress. Oratory was so important to the study of the past because oratory confirmed that eloquently expressed ideas were what mattered most in history. That Columbus destroyed Indians, Washington held slaves, or Puritans persecuted their neighbors seemed beside the point. How do these selections compare with the history that you were taught in school?

F. M. FINCH

The Blue and the Gray

1. By the flow of the inland river,
 Whence the fleets of iron have fled,
Where the blades of the grave-grass quiver,
 Asleep are the ranks of the dead;—
  Under the sod and the dew,
   Waiting the judgment day;
  Under the one, the Blue;
   Under the other, the Gray.

2. These, in the robings of glory,
 Those, in the gloom of defeat,
All, with the battle-blood gory,
 In the dusk of eternity meet;—
  Under the sod and the dew,
   Waiting the judgment day;
  Under the laurel, the Blue;
   Under the willow, the Gray.

3. From the silence of sorrowful hours,
 The desolate mourners go,
Lovingly laden with flowers,
 Alike for the friend and the foe;—
  Under the sod and the dew,
   Waiting the judgment day;
  Under the roses, the Blue;
   Under the lilies, the Gray.

4. So, with an equal splendor,
 The morning sun-rays fall,
With a touch, impartially tender,
 On the blossoms blooming for all;—
  Under the sod and the dew,
   Waiting the judgment day;
  Broidered with gold, the Blue;
   Mellowed with gold, the Gray.

F. M. Finch, "The Blue and the Gray," Lesson 58, in *McGuffey's Fifth Eclectic Reader,* ed. William Holmes McGuffey (New York: American Book Company, 1879), 183–85.

5. So, when the summer calleth,
 On forest and field of grain,
With an equal murmur falleth
 The cooling drip of the rain;—
 Under the sod and the dew,
 Waiting the judgment day;
 Wet with the rain, the Blue;
 Wet with the rain, the Gray.

6. Sadly, but not with upbraiding,
 The generous deed was done;
In the storm of the years that are fading,
 No braver battle was won;—
 Under the sod and the dew,
 Waiting the judgment day;
 Under the blossoms, the Blue;
 Under the garlands, the Gray.

7. No more shall the war-cry sever,
 Or the winding rivers be red;
They banish our anger forever,
 When they laurel the graves of our dead;—
 Under the sod and the dew,
 Waiting the judgment day;
 Love and tears, for the Blue;
 Tears and love, for the Gray.

PATRICK HENRY

Speech before the Virginia Convention

It is natural for man to indulge in the illusions of hope. We are apt to shut our eyes against a painful truth, and listen to the song of that siren till she transforms us into beasts. Is this the part of wise men, engaged in a great and arduous struggle for liberty? Are we disposed to be of the num-

Patrick Henry, "Speech before the Virginia Convention," Lesson 19, in *McGuffey's Sixth Eclectic Reader,* ed. William Holmes McGuffey (New York: American Book Company, 1879), 115–18.

ber of those, who, having eyes, see not, and having ears, hear not the things which so nearly concern their temporal salvation? For my part, whatever anguish of spirit it may cost, I am willing to know the whole truth; to know the worst, and to provide for it.

I have but one lamp by which my feet are guided; and that is the lamp of experience. I know of no way of judging of the future but by the past; and, judging by the past, I wish to know what there has been in the conduct of the British ministry for the last ten years to justify those hopes with which gentlemen have been pleased to solace themselves and the house? Is it that insidious smile with which our petition has been lately received? Trust it not: it will prove a snare to your feet. Suffer not yourselves to be betrayed with a kiss. Ask yourselves, how this gracious reception of our petition comports with those warlike preparations which cover our waters and darken our land. Are fleets and armies necessary to a work of love and reconciliation? Have we shown ourselves so unwilling to be reconciled that force must be called in to win back our love? Let us not deceive ourselves. These are the implements of war and subjugation,—the last arguments to which kings resort.

I ask, gentlemen, what means this martial array, if its purpose be not to force us into submission? Can gentlemen assign any other possible motive for it? Has Great Britain any enemy in this quarter of the world, to call for all this accumulation of navies and armies? No, she has none. They are meant for us: they can be meant for no other. They are sent over to bind and rivet upon us those chains which the British ministry have been so long forging. And what have we to oppose to them? Shall we try argument? We have been trying that for the last ten years. Have we any thing new to offer upon the subject? Nothing. We have held the subject up in every light in which it was capable; but it has been all in vain.

Shall we resort to entreaty and humble supplication? What terms shall we find which have not been already exhausted? Let us not, I beseech you, deceive ourselves longer. We have done every thing that could be done, to avert the storm which is now coming on. We have petitioned; we have remonstrated; we have supplicated; we have prostrated ourselves at the foot of the throne, and implored its interposition to arrest the tyrannical hands of the ministry and parliament. Our petitions have been slighted; our remonstrances have produced additional violence and insult; our supplications disregarded; and we have been spurned with contempt from the foot of the throne.

In vain, after these things, may we indulge the fond hope of peace and reconciliation. There is no longer any room for hope. If we wish to be free; if we mean to preserve inviolate those inestimable privileges for which we have been so long contending; if we mean not basely to abandon the noble struggle in which we have been so long engaged, and which we have pledged ourselves never to abandon until the glorious object of our contest shall be obtained—we must fight! I repeat it, we must fight! An appeal to arms and the God of Hosts, is all that is left us.

They tell us that we are weak; unable to cope with so formidable an adversary. But when shall we be stronger? Will it be the next week, or the next year? Will it be when we are totally disarmed, and when a British guard shall be stationed in every house? Shall we gather strength by irresolution and inaction? Shall we acquire the means of effectual resistance by lying supinely on our backs, and hugging the delusive phantom of hope, until our enemies shall have bound us hand and foot? We are not weak, if we make a proper use of those means which the God of nature hath placed in our power.

Three millions of people, armed in the holy cause of liberty, and in such a country as that which we possess, are invincible by any force which our enemy can send against us. Besides, we shall not fight our battles alone. There is a just God who presides over the destinies of nations; and who will raise up friends to fight our battles for us. The battle is not to the strong alone; it is to the vigilant, the active, the brave. Besides, we have no election. If we were base enough to desire it, it is now too late to retire from the contest. There is no retreat but in submission and slavery! Our chains are forged. Their clanking may be heard on the plains of Boston! The war is inevitable; and, let it come! I repeat it, let it come!

It is in vain to extenuate the matter. Gentlemen may cry peace, peace; but there is no peace. The war is actually begun. The next gale that sweeps from the north, will bring to our ears the clash of resounding arms! Our brethren are already in the field! Why stand we here idle? What is it that gentlemen wish? What would they have? Is life so dear, or peace so sweet, as to be purchased at the price of chains and slavery? Forbid it, Almighty God! I know not what course others may take; but as for me, give me liberty, or give me death.

WASHINGTON IRVING

Character of Columbus

Columbus was a man of great and inventive genius. The operations of his mind were energetic, but irregular; bursting forth, at times, with that irresistible force which characterizes intellect of such an order. His ambition was lofty and noble, inspiring him with high thoughts and an anxiety to distinguish himself by great achievements. He aimed at dignity and wealth in the same elevated spirit with which he sought renown; they were to rise from the territories he should discover, and be commensurate in importance.

His conduct was characterized by the grandeur of his views and the magnanimity of his spirit. Instead of ravaging the newly-found countries, like many of his contemporary discoverers, who were intent only on immediate gain, he regarded them with the eyes of a legislator; he sought to colonize and cultivate them, to civilize the natives, to build cities, introduce the useful arts, subject every thing to the control of law, order, and religion, and thus to found regular and prosperous empires. That he failed in this was the fault of the dissolute rabble which it was his misfortune to command, with whom all law was tyranny and all order oppression.

He was naturally irascible and impetuous, and keenly sensible to injury and injustice; yet the quickness of his temper was counteracted by the generosity and benevolence of his heart. The magnanimity of his nature shone forth through all the troubles of his stormy career. Though continually outraged in his dignity, braved in his authority, foiled in his plans, and endangered in his person by the seditions of turbulent and worthless men, and that, too, at times when suffering under anguish of body and anxiety of mind enough to exasperate the most patient, yet he restrained his valiant and indignant spirit, and brought himself to forbear, and reason, and even to supplicate. Nor can the reader of the story of his eventful life fail to notice how free he was from all feeling of revenge, how ready to forgive and forget on the least sign of repentance and atonement. He has been exalted for his skill in controlling others, but far greater praise is due to him for the firmness he displayed in governing himself.

His piety was genuine and fervent. Religion mingled with the whole

---

Washington Irving, "Character of Columbus," Lesson 47, in *McGuffey's Sixth Eclectic Reader,* ed. William Holmes McGuffey (New York: American Book Company, 1879), 192–95.

course of his thoughts and actions, and shone forth in his most private and unstudied writings. Whenever he made any great discovery he devoutly returned thanks to God. The voice of prayer and the melody of praise rose from his ships on discovering the new world, and his first action on landing was to prostrate himself upon the earth and offer up thanksgiving. All his great enterprises were undertaken in the name of the Holy Trinity, and he partook of the holy sacrament previous to embarkation. He observed the festivals of the church in the wildest situations. The Sabbath was to him a day of sacred rest, on which he would never sail from a port unless in case of extreme necessity. The religion thus deeply seated in his soul diffused a sober dignity and a benign composure over his whole deportment; his very language was pure and guarded, and free from all gross or irreverent expressions.

A peculiar trait in his rich and varied character remains to be noticed; namely, that ardent and enthusiastic imagination which threw a magnificence over his whole course of thought. A poetical temperament is discernible throughout all his writings and in all his actions. We see it in all his descriptions of the beauties of the wild land he was discovering, in the enthusiasm with which he extolled the blandness of the temperature, the purity of the atmosphere, the fragrance of the air, "full of dew and sweetness," the verdure of the forests, the grandeur of the mountains, and the crystal purity of the running streams. It spread a glorious and golden world around him, and tinged every thing with its own gorgeous colors.

With all the visionary fervor of his imagination, its fondest dreams fell short of the reality. He died in ignorance of the real grandeur of his discovery. Until his last breath, he entertained the idea that he had merely opened a new way to the old resorts of opulent commerce, and had discovered some of the wild regions of the East. What visions of glory would have broken upon his mind could he have known that he had indeed discovered a new continent equal to the old world in magnitude, and separated by two vast oceans from all the earth hitherto known by civilized man! How would his magnanimous spirit have been consoled amid the afflictions of age and the cares of penury, the neglect of a fickle public and the injustice of an ungrateful king, could he have anticipated the splendid empires which would arise in the beautiful world he had discovered, and the nations, and tongues, and languages which were to fill its land with his renown, and to revere and bless his name to the latest posterity!

CHARLES SPRAGUE

North American Indians

Not many generations ago, where you now sit, encircled with all that exalts and embellishes civilized life, the rank thistle nodded in the wind and the wild fox dug his hole unscared. Here lived and loved another race of beings. Beneath the same sun that rolls over your head, the Indian hunter pursued the panting deer; gazing on the same moon that smiles for you, the Indian lover wooed his dusky mate. Here the wigwam blaze beamed on the tender and helpless, and the council-fire glared on the wise and daring. Now they dipped their noble limbs in your sedgy lakes, and now they paddled the light canoe along your rocky shores. Here they warred; the echoing whoop, the bloody grapple, the defying death-song, all were here; and when the tiger-strife was over, here curled the smoke of peace.

Here, too, they worshiped; and from many a dark bosom went up a fervent prayer to the Great Spirit. He had not written his laws for them on tables of stone, but he had traced them on the tables of their hearts. The poor child of nature knew not the God of Revelation, but the God of the universe he acknowledged in every thing around. He beheld him in the star that sank in beauty behind his lonely dwelling; in the sacred orb that flamed on him from his midday throne; in the flower that snapped in the morning breeze; in the lofty pine that defied a thousand whirlwinds; in the timid warbler that never left its native grove; in the fearless eagle, whose untired pinion was wet in clouds; in the worm that crawled at his feet; and in his own matchless form, glowing with a spark of that light, to whose mysterious source he bent in humble though blind adoration.

And all this has passed away. Across the ocean came a pilgrim bark, bearing the seeds of life and death. The former were sown for you; the latter sprang up in the path of the simple native. Two hundred years have changed the character of a great continent, and blotted forever from its face a whole, peculiar people. Art has usurped the bowers of nature, and the anointed children of education have been too powerful for the tribes of the ignorant. Here and there a stricken few remain; but how unlike their bold, untamable progenitors. The Indian of falcon glance and lion bearing, the theme of the touching ballad, the hero of the pathetic tale is

---

Charles Sprague, "North American Indians," Lesson 52, in *McGuffey's Sixth Eclectic Reader,* ed. William Holmes McGuffey (New York: American Book Company, 1879), 209–11.

gone, and his degraded offspring crawls upon the soil where he walked in majesty, to remind us how miserable is man when the foot of the conqueror is on his neck.

As a race they have withered from the land. Their arrows are broken, their springs are dried up, their cabins are in the dust. Their council-fire has long since gone out on the shore, and their war-cry is fast fading to the untrodden west. Slowly and sadly they climb the distant mountains, and read their doom in the setting sun. They are shrinking before the mighty tide which is pressing them away; they must soon hear the roar of the last wave which will settle over them forever. Ages hence, the inquisitive white man, as he stands by some growing city, will ponder on the structure of their disturbed remains, and wonder to what manner of persons they belonged. They will live only in the songs and chronicles of their exterminators. Let these be faithful to their rude virtues as men, and pay due tribute to their unhappy fate as a people.

F. W. P. GREENWOOD

Character of the Puritan Fathers of New England

One of the most prominent features which distinguished our forefathers, was their determined resistance to oppression. They seemed born and brought up for the high and special purpose of showing to the world that the civil and religious rights of man—the rights of self-government, of conscience, and independent thought—are not merely things to be talked of and woven into theories, but to be adopted with the whole strength and ardor of the mind, and felt in the profoundest recesses of the heart, and carried out into the general life, and made the foundation of practical usefulness, and visible beauty, and true nobility.

Liberty, with them, was an object of too serious desire and stern resolve to be personified, allegorized, and enshrined. They made no goddess of it, as the ancients did; they had no time nor inclination for such trifling; they felt that liberty was the simple birthright of every human

F. W. P. Greenwood, "Character of the Puritan Fathers of New England," Lesson 57, in *McGuffey's Sixth Eclectic Reader,* ed. William Holmes McGuffey (New York: American Book Company, 1879), 223–26.

creature; they called it so; they claimed it as such; they reverenced and held it fast as the unalienable gift of the Creator, which was not to be surrendered to power, nor sold for wages.

It was theirs, as men; without it, they did not esteem themselves men; more than any other privilege or possession, it was essential to their happiness, for it was essential to their original nature; and therefore they preferred it above wealth, and ease, and country; and, that they might enjoy and exercise it fully, they forsook houses, and lands, and kindred, their homes, their native soil, and their fathers' graves.

They left all these; they left England, which, whatever it might have been called, was not to them a land of freedom; they launched forth on the pathless ocean, the wide, fathomless ocean, soiled not by the earth beneath, and bounded, all round and above, only by heaven; and it seemed to them like that better and sublimer freedom, which their country knew not, but of which they had the conception and image in their hearts; and, after a toilsome and painful voyage, they came to a hard and wintry coast, unfruitful and desolate, but unguarded and boundless; its calm silence interrupted not the ascent of their prayers; it had no eyes to watch, no ears to hearken, no tongues to report of them; here, again, there was an answer to their soul's desire, and they were satisfied, and gave thanks; they saw that they were free, and the desert smiled.

I am telling an old tale; but it is one which must be told when we speak of those men. It is to be added, that they transmitted their principles to their children, and that, peopled by such a race, our country was always free. So long as its inhabitants were unmolested by the mother-country in the exercise of their important rights, they submitted to the form of English government; but when those rights were invaded, they spurned even the form away.

This act was the Revolution, which came of course and spontaneously, and had nothing in it of the wonderful or unforeseen. The wonder would have been if it had not occurred. It was, indeed, a happy and glorious event, but by no means unnatural; and I intend no slight to the revered actors in the Revolution when I assert that their fathers before them were as free as they—every whit as free.

The principles of the Revolution were not the suddenly acquired property of a few bosoms: they were abroad in the land in the ages before; they had always been taught, like the truths of the Bible; they had descended from father to son, down from those primitive days, when the Pilgrim, established in his simple dwelling, and seated at his blazing fire, piled high from the forest which shaded his door, repeated to his listening children the story of his wrongs and his resistance, and bade them rejoice, though the wild winds and the wild beasts were howling without, that they had nothing to fear from great men's oppression.

Here are the beginnings of the Revolution. Every settler's hearth was a school of independence; the scholars were apt, and the lessons sunk deeply; and thus it came that our country was always free; it could not be other than free.

As deeply seated as was the principle of liberty and resistance to arbitrary power in the breasts of the Puritans, it was not more so than their piety and sense of religious obligation. They were emphatically a people whose God was the Lord. Their form of government was as strictly theocratical, if direct communication be excepted, as was that of the Jews; insomuch that it would be difficult to say where there was any civil authority among them entirely distinct from ecclesiastical jurisdiction.

Whenever a few of them settled a town, they immediately gathered themselves into a church; and their elders were magistrates, and their code of laws was the Pentateuch. These were forms, it is true, but forms which faithfully indicated principles and feelings; for no people could have adopted such forms, who were not thoroughly imbued with the spirit, and bent on the practice, of religion.

God was their King; and they regarded him as truly and literally so, as if he had dwelt in a visible palace in the midst of their state. They were his devoted, resolute, humble subjects; they understood nothing which they did not beg of him to prosper; they accomplished nothing without rendering to him the praise; they suffered nothing without carrying their sorrows to his throne; they ate nothing which they did not implore him to bless.

Their piety was not merely external; it was sincere; it had the proof of a good tree in bearing good fruit; it produced and sustained a strict morality. Their tenacious purity of manners and speech obtained for them, in the mother-country, their name of Puritans, which, though given in derision, was as honorable an appellation as was ever bestowed by man on man.

That there were hypocrites among them, is not to be doubted; but they were rare. The men who voluntarily exiled themselves to an unknown coast, and endured there every toil and hardship for conscience' sake, and that they might serve God in their own manner, were not likely to set conscience at defiance, and make the service of God a mockery; they were not likely to be, neither were they, hypocrites. I do not know that it would be arrogating too much for them to say, that, on the extended surface of the globe, there was not a single community of men to be compared with them, in the respects of deep religious impressions and an exact performance of moral duty.

DANIEL WEBSTER

Importance of the Union

Mr. President: I am conscious of having detained you and the Senate much too long. I was drawn into the debate with no previous deliberation, such as is suited to the discussion of so grave and important a subject. But it is a subject of which my heart is full, and I have not been willing to suppress the utterance of its spontaneous sentiments. I can not, even now, persuade myself to relinquish it, without expressing once more my deep conviction, that, since it respects nothing less than the union of the states, it is of most vital and essential importance to the public happiness.

I profess, sir, in my career hitherto, to have kept steadily in view the prosperity and honor of the whole country, and the preservation of our federal Union. It is to that Union we owe our safety at home, and our consideration and dignity abroad. It is to that Union that we are chiefly indebted for whatever makes us most proud of our country. That Union we reached only by the discipline of our virtues, in the severe school of adversity. It had its origin in the necessities of disordered finance, prostrate commerce, and ruined credit. Under its benign influences, these great interests immediately awoke, as from the dead, and sprang forth with newness of life. Every year of its duration has teemed with fresh proofs of its utility and its blessings; and, although our territory has stretched out wider and wider, and our population spread farther and farther, they have not outrun its protection or its benefits. It has been to us all a copious fountain of national, social, and personal happiness.

I have not allowed myself, sir, to look beyond the Union, to see what might lie hidden in the dark recess behind. I have not coolly weighed the chances of preserving liberty, when the bonds that unite us together shall be broken asunder. I have not accustomed myself to hang over the precipice of disunion, to see whether, with my short sight, I can fathom the depth of the abyss below; nor could I regard him as a safe counselor in the affairs of this government, whose thoughts should be mainly bent on considering, not how the Union should be best preserved, but how tolerable might be the condition of the people when it shall be broken up and destroyed.

Daniel Webster, "Importance of the Union," Lesson 102, in *McGuffey's Sixth Eclectic Reader,* ed. William Holmes McGuffey (New York: American Book Company, 1879), 362–64.

While the Union lasts, we have high, exciting, gratifying prospects spread out before us, for us and our children. Beyond that, I seek not to penetrate the veil. God grant that in my day, at least, that curtain may not rise. God grant that on my vision never may be opened what lies behind. When my eyes shall be turned to behold, for the last time, the sun in heaven, may I not see him shining on the broken and dishonored fragments of a once glorious Union; on States dissevered, discordant, belligerent; on a land rent with civil feuds, or drenched, it may be, in fraternal blood.

Let their last feeble and lingering glance rather behold the gorgeous ensign of the Republic, now known and honored throughout the earth, still full high advanced; its arms and trophies streaming in their original luster, not a stripe erased or polluted, not a single star obscured—bearing for its motto no such miserable interrogatory as, What is all this worth? nor those other words of delusion and folly, Liberty first, and Union afterwards—but everywhere, spread all over in characters of living light, blazing on all its ample folds, as they float over the sea and over the land, and in every wind under the whole heavens, that other sentiment, dear to every true American heart—Liberty and Union, now and forever, one and inseparable!

GENERAL HENRY LEE

Eulogy on Washington

Who is there that has forgotten the vales of Brandywine, the fields of Germantown, or the plains of Monmouth?[1] Every-where present, wants of every kind obstructing, numerous and valiant armies encountering, himself a host, he assuaged our sufferings, limited our privations, and upheld our tottering Republic. Shall I display to you the spread of the fire of his soul by rehearsing the praises of the hero of Saratoga, and his much-loved compeer of the Carolinas? No; our Washington wears not borrowed glory. To Gates—to Greene, he gave without reserve the applause due to their

[1]Battle sites of the American Revolution.

General Henry Lee, "Eulogy on Washington," Lesson 131, in *McGuffey's Sixth Eclectic Reader,* ed. William Holmes McGuffey (New York: American Book Company, 1879), 444–45.

eminent merit; and long may the chiefs of Saratoga and of Eutaw receive the grateful respect of a grateful people.[2]

Moving in his own orbit, he imparted heat and light to his most distant satellites; and, combining the physical and moral force of all within his sphere, with irresistible weight he took his course, commiserating folly, disdaining vice, dismaying treason, and invigorating despondency; until the auspicious hour arrived, when, united with the intrepid forces of a potent and magnanimous ally, he brought to submission Cornwallis,[3] since the conqueror of India; thus finishing his long career of military glory with a luster corresponding to his great name, and in this his last act of war, affixing the seal of fate to our nation's birth.

First in war, first in peace, and first in the hearts of his countrymen, he was second to none in humble and endearing scenes of private life. Pious, just, humane, temperate, sincere, uniform, dignified, and commanding, his example was edifying to all around him, as were the effects of that example lasting.

To his equals, he was condescending; to his inferiors, kind; and to the dear object of his affections, exemplarily tender. Correct throughout, vice shuddered in his presence, and virtue always felt his fostering hand; the purity of his private character gave effulgence to his public virtues.

His last scene comported with the whole tenor of his life. Although in extreme pain, not a sigh, not a groan, escaped him; and with undisturbed serenity he closed his well-spent life. Such was the man America has lost! Such was the man for whom our nation mourns!

[2]Patriot Generals Horatio Gates (c. 1728–1806) and Nathanael Greene (1742–1786) won important Revolutionary War battles at Saratoga and Eutaw Springs, respectively.

[3]Lieutenant-General Charles Cornwallis (1738–1805) commanded the English armies in America during the Revolutionary War. He was forced to surrender to a combined French and American army at the siege of Yorktown, effectively ending the war.

12
Literature

Like history, literature was not studied as a distinct subject by nineteenth-century students. Many critics, in fact, believed that America was too new and too raw to produce great writing. The sixth McGuffey reader moved decisively toward including more literature, especially from American writers. Studying literature served several purposes. Soliloquies and poetry were perfect vehicles for students to practice their elocution. Literature also incorporated the Victorian cultural ideal of "the best that was thought and said," and familiarity with the great writers became a mark of status in society. The readers helped make writers like Edgar Allan Poe, William Cullen Bryant, and Henry Wadsworth Longfellow canonical, such that their work continued to be anthologized through the next century. Note in the lessons that follow the repetition of old themes, such as the innocence of childhood, rural nostalgia, and a fascination with death. Why do you think much of this literature is so sentimental in style?

SAMUEL WOODWORTH
The Old Oaken Bucket

1. How dear to this heart are the scenes of my childhood,
   When fond recollection presents them to view!
   The orchard, the meadow, the deep tangled wild-wood,
   And every loved spot which my infancy knew;
   The wide-spreading pond, and the mill that stood by it:

Samuel Woodworth, "The Old Oaken Bucket," Lesson 72, in *McGuffey's Fourth Eclectic Reader,* ed. William Holmes McGuffey (New York: American Book Company, 1879), 202–3.

The bridge and the rock where the cataract fell:
The cot of my father, the dairy-house nigh it,
And e'en the rude bucket which hung in the well:
The old oaken bucket, the iron-bound bucket,
The moss-covered bucket which hung in the well.

2. That moss-covered vessel I hail as a treasure;
   For often, at noon, when returned from the field,
 I found it the source of an exquisite pleasure,
   The purest and sweetest that nature can yield.
 How ardent I seized it, with hands that were glowing,
   And quick to the white-pebbled bottom it fell;
 Then soon, with the emblem of truth overflowing,
   And dripping with coolness, it rose from the well:
 The olden oaken bucket, the iron-bound bucket,
   The moss-covered bucket arose from the well.

3. How sweet from the green mossy brim to receive it,
   As poised on the curb, it inclined to my lips!
 Not a full blushing goblet could tempt me to leave it,
   Though filled with the nectar which Jupiter sips;
 And now, far removed from thy loved situation,
   The tear of regret will intrusively swell,
 As fancy reverts to my father's plantation,
   And sighs for the bucket which hangs in the well:
 The old oaken bucket, the iron-bound bucket,
   The moss-covered bucket, which hangs in the well.

CHARLES DICKENS

Death of Little Nell

She was dead. No sleep so beautiful and calm, so free from trace of pain, so fair to look upon. She seemed a creature fresh from the hand of God, and waiting for the breath of life; not one who had lived, and suffered death. Her couch was dressed with here and there some winter berries and green leaves, gathered in a spot she had been used to favor. "When I die, put near me something that has loved the light, and had the sky above it always." These were her words.

She was dead. Dear, gentle, patient, noble Nell was dead. Her little

Charles Dickens, "Death of Little Nell," Lesson 13, in *McGuffey's Sixth Eclectic Reader,* ed. William Holmes McGuffey (New York: American Book Company, 1879), 96–100.

bird, a poor, slight thing the pressure of a finger would have crushed, was stirring nimbly in its cage, and the strong heart of its child-mistress was mute and motionless forever! Where were the traces of her early cares, her sufferings, and fatigues? All gone. Sorrow was dead, indeed, in her; but peace and perfect happiness were born, imagined in her tranquil beauty and profound repose.

And still her former self lay there, unaltered in this change. Yes! the old fireside had smiled upon that same sweet face; it had passed, like a dream, through haunts of misery and care; at the door of the poor school-master on the summer evening, before the furnace fire upon the cold wet night, at the still bedside of the dying boy, there had been the same mild and lovely look. So shall we know the angels, in their majesty, after death.

The old man held one languid arm in his, and had the small hand tight folded to his breast for warmth. It was the hand she had stretched out to him with her last smile; the hand that had led him on through all their wanderings. Ever and anon he pressed it to his lips; then hugged it to his breast again, murmuring that it was warmer now, and, as he said it, he looked in agony to those who stood around, as if imploring them to help her.

She was dead, and past all help, or need of help. The ancient rooms she had seemed to fill with life, even while her own was waning fast, the garden she had tended, the eyes she had gladdened, the noiseless haunts of many a thoughtful hour, the paths she had trodden, as it were, but yesterday, could know her no more.

"It is not," said the school-master, as he bent down to kiss her on the cheek, and gave his tears free vent, "it is not in *this* world that heaven's justice ends. Think what earth is, compared with the world to which her young spirit has winged its early flight, and say, if one deliberate wish, expressed in solemn tones above this bed, could call her back to life, which of us would utter it?"

She had been dead two days. They were all about her at the time, knowing that the end was drawing on. She died soon after day-break. They had read and talked to her in the earlier portion of the night; but, as the hours crept on, she sank to sleep. They could tell by what she faintly uttered in her dreams, that they were of her journeyings with the old man; they were of no painful scenes, but of people who had helped them, and used them kindly; for she often said "God bless you!" with great fervor.

Waking, she never wandered in her mind but once, and that was at beautiful music, which, she said, was in the air. God knows. It may have been. Opening her eyes, at last, from a very quiet sleep, she begged that they would kiss her once again. That done, she turned to the old man, with a lovely smile upon her face, such, they said, as they had never seen, and could never forget, and clung, with both her arms, about his neck. She had never murmured or complained; but, with a quiet mind, and manner quite unaltered, save that she every day became more earnest and more grateful to them, faded like the light upon the summer's evening.

The child who had been her little friend, came there, almost as soon as it was day, with an offering of dried flowers, which he begged them to lay upon her breast. He told them of his dream again, and that it was of her being restored to them, just as she used to be. He begged hard to see her: saying, that he would be very quiet, and that they need not fear his being alarmed, for he had sat alone by his young brother all day long, when he was dead, and had felt glad to be so near him. They let him have his wish; and, indeed, he kept his word, and was, in his childish way, a lesson to them all.

Up to that time, the old man had not spoken once, except to her, or stirred from the bedside. But, when he saw her little favorite, he was moved as they had not seen him yet, and made as though he would have him come nearer. Then, pointing to the bed, he burst into tears for the first time, and they who stood by, knowing that the sight of this child had done him good, left them alone together.

Soothing him with his artless talk of her, the child persuaded him to take some rest, to walk abroad, to do almost as he desired him. And, when the day came, on which they must remove her, in her earthly shape, from earthly eyes forever, he led him away, that he might not know when she was taken from him. They were to gather fresh leaves and berries for her bed.

And now the bell, the bell she had so often heard by night and day, and listened to with solemn pleasure, almost as a living voice, rung its remorseless toll for her, so young, so beautiful, so good. Decrepit age, and vigorous life, and blooming youth, and helpless infancy,—on crutches, in the pride of health and strength, in the full blush of promise, in the mere dawn of life, gathered round her. Old men were there, whose eyes were dim and senses failing, grandmothers, who might have died ten years ago, and still been old, the deaf, the blind, the lame, the palsied, the living dead, in many shapes and forms, to see the closing of that early grave.

Along the crowded path they bore her now, pure as the newly fallen snow that covered it, whose day on earth had been as fleeting. Under that porch, where she had sat when heaven, in its mercy, brought her to that peaceful spot, she passed again, and the old church received her in its quiet shade.

WASHINGTON IRVING

Rip Van Winkle

The appearance of Rip, with his long, grizzled beard, his rusty fowling-piece, his uncouth dress, and an army of women and children at his heels, soon attracted the attention of the tavern politicians. They crowded around him, eying him from head to foot with great curiosity. The orator bustled up to him, and, drawing him partly aside, inquired on which side he voted. Rip stared in vacant stupidity. Another short but busy little fellow pulled him by the arm, and, rising on tiptoe, inquired in his ear "whether he was Federal or Democrat."

Rip was equally at a loss to comprehend the question; when a knowing, self-important old gentleman, in a sharp cocked hat, made his way through the crowd, putting them to the right and left with his elbows as he passed, and planting himself before Van Winkle, with one arm akimbo, the other resting on his cane, his keen eyes and sharp hat penetrating, as it were, into his very soul, demanded, in an austere tone, what brought him to the election with a gun on his shoulder, and a mob at his heels, and whether he meant to breed a riot in the village.

"Alas! gentlemen," cried Rip, somewhat dismayed, "I am a poor, quiet man, a native of the place, and a loyal subject of the king, God bless him!" Here a general shout burst from the bystanders.—"A tory! a tory! a spy! a refugee! hustle him! away with him!" It was with great difficulty that the self-important man in the cocked hat restored order; and, having a tenfold austerity of brow, demanded again of the unknown culprit, what he came there for, and whom he was seeking. The poor man humbly assured him that he meant no harm, but merely came there in search of some of his neighbors, who used to keep about the tavern. "Well, who are they? name them."

Rip bethought himself a moment, and inquired, "Where's Nicholas

Washington Irving, "Rip Van Winkle," Lesson 63, in *McGuffey's Sixth Eclectic Reader,* ed. William Holmes McGuffey (New York: American Book Company, 1879), 242–45.

Vedder?" There was a silence for a little while, when an old man replied, in a thin, piping voice, "Nicholas Vedder! why he is dead and gone these eighteen years! There was a wooden tombstone in the church-yard that used to tell all about him, but that's rotten and gone too." "Where's Brom Dutcher?" "Oh, he went off to the army in the beginning of the war. Some say he was killed at the storming of Stony Point; others say he was drowned in a squall at the foot of Anthony's Nose. I don't know; he never came back again."

"Where's Van Bummel, the schoolmaster?" "He went off to the wars, too; was a great militia general, and is now in Congress." Rip's heart died away at hearing of these sad changes in his home and friends, and finding himself thus alone in the world. Every answer puzzled him, too, by treating of such enormous lapses of time, and of matters which he could not understand—war, Congress, Stony Point. He had no courage to ask after any more friends, but cried out in despair, "Does nobody here know Rip Van Winkle?"

"Oh, Rip Van Winkle!" exclaimed two or three. "Oh, to be sure! That's Rip Van Winkle yonder, leaning against the tree." Rip looked, and beheld a precise counterpart of himself as he went up the mountain; apparently as lazy, and certainly as ragged. The poor fellow was now completely confounded; he doubted his own identity, and whether he was himself or another man. In the midst of his bewilderment, the man in the cocked hat demanded who he was, and what was his name.

"God knows!" exclaimed he, at his wit's end. "I'm not myself; I'm somebody else; that's me yonder; no, that's somebody else got into my shoes. I was myself last night; but I fell asleep on the mountain, and they've changed my gun, and every thing's changed, and I'm changed, and I can't tell what's my name or who I am!"

The by-standers began now to look at each other, nod, wink significantly, and tap their fingers against their foreheads. There was a whisper, also, about securing the gun, and keeping the old fellow from doing mischief, at the very suggestion of which the self-important man in the cocked hat retired with some precipitation. At this critical moment, a fresh, comely woman pressed through the throng to get a peep at the gray-bearded man. She had a chubby child in her arms, which, frightened at his looks, began to cry. "Hush, Rip!" cried she, "hush, you little fool! the old man won't hurt you."

The name of the child, the air of the mother, the tone of her voice, all awakened a train of recollections in his mind. "What is your name, my good woman?" asked he. "Judith Gardenier." "And your father's name?" "Ah, poor man! Rip Van Winkle was his name; but it's twenty years since he went away from home with his gun, and never has been heard of since; his dog came home without him; but whether he shot himself, or was carried away by the Indians, nobody can tell. I was then but a little girl."

Rip had but one question more to ask; but he put it with a faltering voice: "Where's your mother?" "Oh, she, too, died but a short time since; she broke a blood-vessel in a fit of passion at a New England peddler." There was a drop of comfort, at least, in this intelligence. The honest man could contain himself no longer. He caught his daughter and her child in his arms. "I am your father!" cried he. "Young Rip Van Winkle once, old Rip Van Winkle now! Does nobody know poor Rip Van Winkle?"

All stood amazed, until an old woman, tottering out from among the crowd, put her hand to her brow, and, peering under it in his face for a moment, exclaimed, "Sure enough! it is Rip Van Winkle! it is himself! Welcome home again, old neighbor! Why, where have you been these twenty long years?" Rip's story was soon told, for the whole twenty years had been to him but as one night.

To make a long story short, the company broke up and returned to the more important concerns of the election. Rip's daughter took him home to live with her. She had a snug, well-furnished house, and a stout, cheery farmer for a husband, whom Rip recollected for one of the urchins that used to climb upon his back. Rip now resumed his old walks and habits. He soon found many of his former cronies, though all rather the worse for the wear and tear of time, and preferred making friends among the rising generation, with whom he soon grew into great favor.

WILLIAM CULLEN BRYANT

Thanatopsis

To him who in the love of Nature holds
Communion with her visible forms, she speaks
A various language: for his gayer hours
She has a voice of gladness, and a smile
And eloquence of beauty; and she glides
Into his darker musings, with a mild

William Cullen Bryant, "Thanatopsis," Lesson 75, in *McGuffey's Sixth Eclectic Reader,* ed. William Holmes McGuffey (New York: American Book Company, 1879), 275–78.

And healing sympathy, that steals away
Their sharpness, ere he is aware.

When thoughts
Of the last bitter hour come like a blight
Over thy spirit, and sad images
Of the stern agony, and shroud, and pall,
And breathless darkness, and the narrow house,
Make thee to shudder, and grow sick at heart;—
Go forth, under the open sky, and list
To Nature's teachings, while from all around—
Earth and her waters, and the depths of air—
Comes a still voice,—

Yet a few days, and thee
The all-beholding sun shall see no more
In all his course; nor yet in the cold ground,
Where thy pale form was laid, with many tears,
Nor in the embrace of ocean, shall exist
Thy image. Earth, that nourished thee, shall claim
Thy growth, to be resolved to earth again;
And, lost each human trace, surrendering up
Thine individual being, shalt thou go
To mix for ever with the elements;
To be a brother to the insensible rock
And to the sluggish clod, which the rude swain
Turns with his share, and treads upon. The oak
Shall send his roots abroad, and pierce thy mold.

Yet not to thine eternal resting-place
Shalt thou retire alone, nor couldst thou wish
Couch more magnificent. Thou shalt lie down
With patriarchs of the infant world,—with kings,
The powerful of the earth,—the wise, the good,
Fair forms, and hoary seers of ages past,—
All in one mighty sepulcher.

The hills,
Rock-ribbed, and ancient as the sun; the vales
Stretching in pensive quietness between;
The venerable woods; rivers that move
In majesty, and the complaining brooks,
That make the meadows green; and, poured round all,
Old Ocean's gray and melancholy waste,—

Are but the solemn decorations all
Of the great tomb of man. The golden sun,
The planets, all the infinite host of heaven,
Are shining on the sad abodes of death,
Through the still lapse of ages.

All that tread
The globe are but a handful to the tribes
That slumber in its bosom. Take the wings
Of morning, pierce the Barcan wilderness,
Or lose thyself in the continuous woods
Where rolls the Oregon, and hears no sound
Save his own dashings,—yet the dead are there:
And millions in those solitudes, since first
The flight of years began, have laid them down
In their last sleep,—the dead reign there alone.

So shalt thou rest; and what if thou withdraw
In silence from the living, and no friend
Take note of thy departure? All that breathe
Will share thy destiny. The gay will laugh
When thou art gone, the solemn brood of care
Plod on, and each one as before will chase
His favorite phantom; yet all these shall leave
Their mirth and their employments, and shall come
And make their bed with thee. As the long train
Of ages glide away, the sons of men—
The youth in life's green spring, and he who goes
In the full strength of years, matron and maid,
The speechless babe, and the gray-headed man—
Shall one by one be gathered to thy side
By those who in their turn shall follow them.

So live, that when thy summons comes to join
The innumerable caravan, which moves
To that mysterious realm, where each shall take
His chamber in the silent halls of death,
Thou go not, like the quarry-slave at night,
Scourged to his dungeon, but, sustained and soothed
By an unfaltering trust, approach thy grave,
Like one who wraps the drapery of his couch
About him, and lies down to pleasant dreams.

JOHN GREENLEAF WHITTIER

The Barefoot Boy

Blessings on thee, little man,
Barefoot boy, with cheek of tan!
With thy turned-up pantaloons,
And thy merry whistled tunes;
With thy red lip, redder still
Kissed by strawberries on the hill;
With the sunshine on thy face,
Through thy torn brim's jaunty grace;
From my heart I give thee joy,—
I was once a barefoot boy!
Prince thou art,—the grown-up man
Only is republican.
Let the million-dollared ride!
Barefoot, trudging at his side,
Thou hast more than he can buy
In the reach of ear and eye,—
Outward sunshine, inward joy:
Blessings on thee, barefoot boy!

Oh for boyhood's painless play,
Sleep that wakes in laughing day,
Health that mocks the doctor's rules,
Knowledge never learned of schools,
Of the wild bee's morning chase,
Of the wild flower's time and place,
Flight of fowl and habitude
Of the tenants of the wood;
How the tortoise bears his shell,
How the woodchuck digs his cell,
And the ground-mole sinks his well;
How the robin feeds her young,
How the oriole's nest is hung;
Where the whitest lilies blow,

John Greenleaf Whittier, "The Barefoot Boy," Lesson 87, in *McGuffey's Sixth Eclectic Reader,* ed. William Holmes McGuffey (New York: American Book Company, 1879), 317–20.

Where the freshest berries grow,
Where the ground-nut trails its vine,
Where the wood-grape's clusters shine;
Of the black wasp's cunning way
Mason of his walls of clay,
And the architectural plans
Of gray hornet artisans!—
For, eschewing books and tasks,
Nature answers all he asks;
Hand in hand with her he walks,
Face to face with her he talks,
Part and parcel of her joy,—
Blessings on thee, barefoot boy!

Oh for boyhood's time of June,
Crowding years in one brief moon,
When all things I heard or saw
Me, their master, waited for.
I was rich in flowers and trees,
Humming-birds and honey-bees;
For my sport the squirrel played,
Plied the snouted mole his spade;
For my taste the blackberry cone
Purpled over hedge and stone;
Laughed the brook for my delight
Through the day and through the night,
Whispering at the garden wall,
Talked with me from fall to fall;
Mine the sand-rimmed pickerel pond,
Mine the walnut slopes beyond,
Mine, on bending orchard trees,
Apples of Hesperides!
Still, as my horizon grew,
Larger grew my riches too;
All the world I saw or knew
Seemed a complex Chinese toy,
Fashioned for a barefoot boy!

Oh for festal dainties spread,
Like my bowl of milk and bread,—
Pewter spoon and bowl of wood,
On the door-stone, gray and rude!

O'er me, like a regal tent,
Cloudy-ribbed, the sunset bent,
Purple-curtained, fringed with gold,
Looped in many a wind-swung fold;
While for music came the play
Of the pied frog's orchestra;
And to light the noisy choir,
Lit the fly his lamp of fire.
I was monarch: pomp and joy
Waited on the barefoot boy!

Cheerily, then, my little man,
Live and laugh, as boyhood can:
Though the flinty slopes be hard,
Stubble-speared the new-mown sward,
Every morn shall lead thee through
Fresh baptisms of the dew;
Every evening from thy feet
Shall the cool wind kiss the heat:
All too soon these feet must hide
In the prison cells of pride,
Lose the freedom of the sod,
Like a colt's for work be shod,
Made to tread the mills of toil,
Up and down in ceaseless moil:
Happy if their track be found
Never on forbidden ground;
Happy if they sink not in
Quick and treacherous sands of sin.
Ah! that thou shouldst know thy joy
Ere it passes, barefoot boy!

WILLIAM SHAKESPEARE

Hamlet's Soliloquy

To be, or not to be; that is the question:—
Whether 'tis nobler in the mind to suffer
The slings and arrows of outrageous fortune,
Or to take arms against a sea of troubles,
And by opposing end them? To die,—to sleep,—
No more: and by a sleep to say we end
The heart-ache and the thousand natural shocks
That flesh is heir to,—'tis a consummation
Devoutly to be wished. To die,—to sleep:—
To sleep! perchance to dream:—ay, there's the rub;
For in that sleep of death what dreams may come
When we have shuffled off this mortal coil,
Must give us pause. There's the respect
That makes calamity of so long life;
For who would bear the whips and scorns of time,
The oppressor's wrong, the proud man's contumely,
The pangs of despisèd love, the law's delay,
The insolence of office, and the spurns
That patient merit of the unworthy takes,
When he himself might his quietus make
With a bare bodkin?[1] Who would fardels[2] bear,
To grunt and sweat under a weary life,
But that the dread of something after death,—
The undiscovered country from whose bourn
No traveler returns,—puzzles the will
And makes us rather bear those ills we have
Than fly to others that we know not of?
Thus conscience doth make cowards of us all;
And thus the native hue of resolution
Is sicklied o'er with the pale cast of thought,

[1]When he might take his own life with a sharp instrument.
[2]Burdens.

William Shakespeare, "Hamlet's Soliloquy (from *Hamlet,* 3.1)," Lesson 94, in *McGuffey's Sixth Eclectic Reader,* ed. William Holmes McGuffey (New York: American Book Company, 1879), 339–40.

And enterprises of great pith and moment
With this regard their currents turn awry,
And lose the name of action.

EDGAR ALLAN POE

The Raven

Once upon a midnight dreary,
While I pondered, weak and weary,
Over many a quaint and curious
Volume of forgotten lore—
While I nodded, nearly napping,
Suddenly there came a tapping,
As of some one gently rapping,
Rapping at my chamber door.
" 'Tis some visitor," I muttered,
"Tapping at my chamber door—
Only this, and nothing more."

Ah, distinctly I remember,
It was in the bleak December,
And each separate dying ember
Wrought its ghost upon the floor.
Eagerly I wished the morrow;—
Vainly I had sought to borrow
From my books surcease of sorrow—
Sorrow for the lost Lenore—
For the rare and radiant maiden
Whom the angels name Lenore—
Nameless here for evermore.

And the silken, sad, uncertain
Rustling of each purple curtain
Thrilled me,—filled me with fantastic
Terrors, never felt before;

Edgar Allan Poe, "The Raven," Lesson 109, in *McGuffey's Sixth Eclectic Reader,* ed. William Holmes McGuffey (New York: American Book Company, 1879), 382–89.

So that now, to still the beating
Of my heart, I stood repeating,
" 'Tis some visitor entreating
Entrance at my chamber door—
Some late visitor entreating
Entrance at my chamber door;
This it is, and nothing more."

Presently my soul grew stronger;
Hesitating then no longer,
"Sir," said I, "or Madam, truly
Your forgiveness I implore;
But the fact is I was napping,
And so gently you came rapping,
And so faintly you came tapping,
Tapping at my chamber door,
That I scarce was sure I heard you."—
Here I opened wide the door;—
Darkness there, and nothing more.

Deep into that darkness peering,
Long I stood there, wondering, fearing,
Doubting, dreaming dreams no mortals
Ever dared to dream before;
But the silence was unbroken,
And the stillness gave no token,
And the only word there spoken
Was the whispered word, "Lenore!"
This I whispered, and an echo
Murmured back the word, "Lenore!"—
Merely this, and nothing more.

Back into the chamber turning,
All my soul within me burning,
Soon again I heard a tapping,
Something louder than before.
"Surely," said I, "surely, that is
Something at my window lattice;
Let me see then, what thereat is,
And this mystery explore—
Let my heart be still a moment,
And this mystery explore;—
'Tis the wind, and nothing more."

Open here I flung the shutter,
When, with many a flirt and flutter,
In there stepped a stately Raven
Of the saintly days of yore;
Not the least obeisance made he;
Not a minute stopped or stayed he,
But, with mien of lord or lady,
Perched above my chamber door—
Perched upon a bust of Pallas[3]
Just above my chamber door—
Perched, and sat, and nothing more.

Then this ebony bird beguiling
My sad fancy into smiling,
By the grave and stern decorum
Of the countenance it wore,
"Though thy crest be shorn and shaven,
Thou," I said, "art sure no craven,
Ghastly, grim, and ancient Raven,
Wandering from the nightly shore,
Tell me what thy lordly name is
On the night's Plutonian shore!"[4]
Quoth the Raven, "Nevermore."

Much I marveled this ungainly
Fowl to hear discourse so plainly,
Though its answer little meaning—
Little relevancy bore;
For we can not help agreeing
That no living human being
Ever yet was blest with seeing
Bird above his chamber door—
Bird or beast upon the sculptured
Bust above his chamber door,
With such name as "Nevermore."

But the Raven, sitting lonely
On that placid bust, spoke only
That one word, as if his soul in

[3]Pallas is another name for the goddess Athena in Greek mythology.
[4]Refers to the infernal regions; hell or Hades in Greek mythology.

That one word he did outpour.
Nothing farther then he uttered,
Not a feather then he fluttered,
Till I scarcely more than muttered,
"Other friends have flown before—
On the morrow he will leave me,
As my Hopes have flown before."
Then the bird said, "Nevermore."

Startled at the stillness broken
By reply so aptly spoken,
"Doubtless," said I, "what it utters
Is its only stock and store,
Caught from some unhappy master
Whom unmerciful Disaster
Followed fast and followed faster
Till his songs one burden bore—
Till the dirges of his Hope that
Melancholy burden bore
Of 'Never—nevermore.' "

But the Raven still beguiling
All my sad soul into smiling,
Straight I wheeled a cushioned seat in
Front of bird, and bust, and door;
Then, upon the velvet sinking,
I betook myself to linking
Fancy unto fancy, thinking
What this ominous bird of yore—
What this grim, ungainly, ghastly,
Gaunt, and ominous bird of yore
Meant in croaking "Nevermore."

This I sat engaged in guessing,
But no syllable expressing
To the fowl whose fiery eyes now
Burned into my bosom's core;
This and more I sat divining,
With my head at ease reclining
On the cushion's velvet lining
That the lamp-light gloated o'er,
But whose velvet violet lining,

With the lamp-light gloating o'er
She shall press, ah, nevermore!

Then, methought, the air grew denser,
Perfumed from an unseen censer[5]
Swung by Seraphim,[6] whose footfalls
Tinkled on the tufted floor.
"Wretch," I cried, "thy God hath lent thee—
By these angels he hath sent thee
Respite—respite and nepenthe
From thy memories of Lenore!
Quaff, oh quaff this kind nepenthe,
And forget this lost Lenore!"
Quoth the Raven, "Nevermore."

"Prophet!" said I, "thing of evil!—
Prophet still, if bird or devil!—
Whether Tempter sent, or whether
Tempest tossed thee here ashore,
Desolate, yet all undaunted,
On this desert land enchanted—
On this home by Horror haunted—
Tell me truly, I implore—
Is there—is there balm in Gilead?
Tell me—tell me, I implore!"
Quoth the Raven, "Nevermore."

"Prophet!" said I, "thing of evil,—
Prophet still, if bird or devil!—
By that heaven that bends above us,
By that God we both adore,
Tell this soul with sorrow laden,
If, within the distant Aidenn,
It shall clasp a sainted maiden
Whom the angels name Lenore—
Clasp a rare and radiant maiden,
Whom the angels name Lenore."
Quoth the Raven, "Nevermore."

[5]Incense holder.
[6]Angels.

"Be that word our sign of parting,
Bird or fiend," I shrieked, upstarting;
"Get thee back into the tempest
And the night's Plutonian shore!
Leave no black plume as a token
Of that lie thy soul hath spoken!
Leave my loneliness unbroken!—
Quit the bust above my door!
Take thy beak from out of my heart, and
Take thy form from off my door!"
Quoth the Raven, "Nevermore."

And the Raven, never flitting,
Still is sitting, still is sitting
On the pallid bust of Pallas
Just above my chamber door;
And his eyes have all the seeming
Of a demon's that is dreaming,
And the lamplight o'er him streaming
Throws his shadow on the floor;
And my soul from out that shadow,
That lies floating on the floor,
Shall be lifted—nevermore!

HENRY WADSWORTH LONGFELLOW

A Psalm of Life

Tell me not, in mournful numbers,
    Life is but an empty dream!
For the soul is dead that slumbers,
    And things are not what they seem.

Life is real! Life is earnest!
    And the grave is not its goal;

Henry Wadsworth Longfellow, "A Psalm of Life," Lesson 125, in *McGuffey's Sixth Eclectic Reader,* ed. William Holmes McGuffey (New York: American Book Company, 1879), 429–30.

Dust thou art, to dust returnest,
Was not spoken of the soul.

Not enjoyment, and not sorrow,
Is our destined end or way;
But to act, that each to-morrow
Find us farther than to-day.

Art is long, and Time is fleeting,
And our hearts, though stout and brave,
Still, like muffled drums, are beating
Funeral marches to the grave.

In the world's broad field of battle,
In the bivouac of Life,
Be not like dumb, driven cattle!
Be a hero in the strife!

Trust no Future, howe'er pleasant!
Let the dead Past bury its dead!
Act—act in the living Present!
Heart within, and God o'erhead.

Lives of great men all remind us
We can make our lives sublime,
And, departing, leave behind us
Foot-prints on the sands of time;—

Foot-prints, that perhaps another,
Sailing o'er life's solemn main,
A forlorn and shipwrecked brother,
Seeing, shall take heart again.

Let us, then, be up and doing,
With a heart for any fate;
Still achieving, still pursuing,
Learn to labor and to wait.

WILLIAM CULLEN BRYANT

Lines to a Water-Fowl

Whither 'midst falling dew,
While glow the heavens with the last steps of day,
Far, through their rosy depths, dost thou pursue
Thy solitary way?

Vainly the fowler's eye
Might mark thy distant flight to do thee wrong,
As, darkly painted on the crimson sky,
Thy figure floats along.

Seek'st thou the plashy brink
Of weedy lake, or marge of river wide,
Or where the rocky billows rise and sink
On the chafed ocean side?

There is a Power whose care
Teaches thy way along that pathless coast,
The desert and illimitable air,
Lone wandering, but not lost.

All day, thy wings have fanned,
At that far height, the cold, thin atmosphere,
Yet stoop not, weary, to the welcome land,
Though the dark night is near.

And soon that toil shall end,
Soon shalt thou find a summer home, and rest,
And scream among thy fellows; reeds shall bend,
Soon, o'er thy sheltered nest.

Thou'rt gone; the abyss of heaven
Hath swallowed up thy form; yet, on my heart,
Deeply has sunk the lesson thou hast given,
And shall not soon depart.

William Cullen Bryant, "Lines to a Water-Fowl," Lesson 127, in *McGuffey's Sixth Eclectic Reader,* ed. William Holmes McGuffey (New York: American Book Company, 1879), 434–35.

He, who, from zone to zone,
Guides through the boundless sky thy certain flight,
In the long way that I must tread alone,
Will lead my steps aright.

A McGuffey Chronology (1800–1941)

1800 William Holmes McGuffey born on September 23 in western Pennsylvania.

1826 McGuffey becomes Professor of Ancient Languages at Miami University, Oxford, Ohio.

1827 McGuffey marries Harriet Spinning on April 3.

1832 First meeting of the Western Literary Institute is held on October 3.

1836–37 Volumes one through four of the Eclectic Readers are published by Cincinnati publisher Truman and Smith.

1841 McGuffey's name first appears in the title when the books' popularity results in a reprinting of original volumes.

1844 *McGuffey's Rhetorical Guide* or fifth reader compiled by Alexander McGuffey and published by W. B. Smith of Cincinnati.

1857 The first major revision of the readers is published under the direction of publisher W. B. Smith of Cincinnati. First version of the sixth reader, compiled by Alexander McGuffey, published with this edition.

1873 William Holmes McGuffey dies on May 4 in Charlottesville, Virginia.

1879 The second major revision of the readers is published under the direction of New York publisher Van Antwerp, Bragg and Co.

1941 McGuffey Memorial is dedicated in Oxford, Ohio.

Questions for Consideration

1. In what ways is God central to humankind in the readers?
2. What attitudes toward American nationhood are expressed in the McGuffeys? What is the nature of patriotism?
3. How do the readers portray various ethnic groups? What are their relationships to each other?
4. What, according to the McGuffeys, constitutes a righteous life?
5. How are girls and women depicted in the readers? Boys and men? How do their social roles differ?
6. In what sense were the McGuffeys appropriate for a market economy?
7. What attitudes toward poverty does the text reveal? Attitudes toward wealth? What responsibilities do rich and poor have toward each other?
8. What relationships do we find here between parents and children? Teachers and students?
9. How would you characterize the style and tone of the selections?
10. What impressions of family life come through in the readers? What obligations do family members have to each other?
11. What attitudes toward crime and deviance are expressed by the McGuffeys? In what way does "immorality" help define proper ways of living?
12. Besides the lessons becoming more difficult, what changes do you find among lessons from the earlier and the later readers?
13. What images of the country and the city are presented in the readers?
14. Why do you think that teaching elocution was so important in nineteenth-century education?
15. What is meant by the phrase "the refinement of America"? How does it relate to the McGuffeys?

Selected Bibliography

Bushman, Richard L. *The Refinement of America: Persons, Houses, Cities.* New York: Random House, 1992.

Cayton, Andrew R. L., and Peter S. Onuf. *The Midwest and the Nation: Rethinking the History of an American Region.* Bloomington: Indiana University Press, 1990.

Cremin, Lawrence A. *American Education, the National Experience, 1783–1876.* New York: Harper and Row, 1980.

Elson, Ruth Miller. *Guardians of Tradition: American Schoolbooks of the Nineteenth Century.* Lincoln: University of Nebraska Press, 1964.

Fuller, Wayne E. *The Old Country School: The Story of Rural Education in the Middle West.* Chicago: University of Chicago Press, 1982.

Havighurst, Walter. *The Miami Years: 1809–1984.* New York: Putnam, 1971.

Kaestle, Carl F. *Pillars of the Republic: Common School and American Society, 1780–1860.* New York: Hill and Wang, 1983.

Lindberg, Stanley W., ed. *The Annotated McGuffey: Selections from the* McGuffey Eclectic Readers, *1836–1920.* New York: Van Nostrand Reinhold, 1976.

McGuffey, William Holmes. Collected correspondence, Walter Havighurst Special Collections, King Library, Miami University, Oxford, Ohio.

McGuffey, William Holmes. *Eclectic First Reader.* Cincinnati: Truman and Smith, 1836.

———. *Eclectic Second Reader.* Cincinnati: Truman and Smith, 1836.

———. *Eclectic Third Reader.* Cincinnati: Truman and Smith, 1837.

———. *Eclectic Fourth Reader.* Cincinnati: Truman and Smith, 1837.

———. *McGuffey's Rhetorical Guide* (fifth reader). Comp. Alexander McGuffey. Cincinnati: W. B. Smith, 1844.

———. *McGuffey's New First Eclectic Reader.* Cincinnati: W. B. Smith, 1857.

———. *McGuffey's New Second Eclectic Reader.* Cincinnati: W. B. Smith, 1857.

———. *McGuffey's New Third Eclectic Reader.* Cincinnati: W. B. Smith, 1857.

———. *McGuffey's New Fourth Eclectic Reader.* Cincinnati: W. B. Smith, 1857.

———. *McGuffey's New Fifth Eclectic Reader.* Cincinnati: W. B. Smith, 1857.

———. *McGuffey's New Sixth Eclectic Reader.* Comp. Alexander McGuffey. Cincinnati: W. B. Smith, 1857.
———. *McGuffey's First Eclectic Reader.* New York: Van Antwerp, Bragg and Co., 1879.
———. *McGuffey's Second Eclectic Reader.* New York: Van Antwerp, Bragg and Co., 1879.
———. *McGuffey's Third Eclectic Reader.* New York: Van Antwerp, Bragg and Co., 1879.
———. *McGuffey's Fourth Eclectic Reader.* New York: Van Antwerp, Bragg and Co., 1879.
———. *McGuffey's Fifth Eclectic Reader.* New York: Van Antwerp, Bragg and Co., 1879.
———. *McGuffey's Sixth Eclectic Reader.* New York: Van Antwerp, Bragg and Co., 1879.
Minnich, Harvey C. *William Holmes McGuffey and His Readers.* New York: American Book Company, 1936.
Mosier, Richard. *Making the American Mind: Social and Moral Ideas in the McGuffey Readers.* New York: Russell and Russell, 1965.
Reese, William J. *The Origins of the American High School.* New Haven: Yale University Press, 1995.
Sullivan, Dolores P. *William Holmes McGuffey, Schoolmaster to the Nation.* Rutherford, N.J.: Fairleigh Dickinson University Press, 1994.
Tyack, David, and Elisabeth Hansot. *Learning Together: A History of Coeducation in American Public Schools.* New Haven: Yale University Press, 1990.
Urban, Wayne, and Jennings Wagoner Jr. *American Education: A History.* New York: McGraw-Hill, 1996.
Vail, Henry. *A History of the McGuffey Readers.* Cleveland: Burrows, 1911.
Westerhoff, John H. *McGuffey and His Readers.* Nashville: Abingdon Press, 1978.

Index